Caution:
I Brake for Plastic Bags

*Grateful for
your
support,*

Anna Willis

10·17·94

Caution:
I Brake for Plastic Bags

REAL-LIFE ENCOURAGEMENT FOR
PARENTS AND FAMILIES

Anna C. Willis

The Upper Room

EDUCATION FOR PARENTING, INC.

1994

Published
in the United States by
THE UPPER ROOM, EDUCATION
FOR PARENTING, INC.,
Derry, New Hampshire.

A portion of this text
was originally published in the Salem Observer
and the Derry News.

Library of Congress Catalog Card Number: 94-90075

IBSN 0-9641087-0-4

Manufactured in the
United States of America
First Edition

*Typeset in Carol Twombly's Adobe Caslon.
Book & cover design by Christopher Willis*

For the love of Robert

Acknowledgments

The encouragement and support for the development of this book
have been astonishing. The following people need to be recognized:

For financial support...
   Maigret Charette and Peter Corrigan, Bob and Maria Dojny, Tom and
   Michele Eberle, Helen and Serge Cryvoff, Mary Kay Frahm, Carol and
   Steve Furstenau, Hampstead Hospital, Thelma Hutton, Gail James,
   Tom Meighan, Lorrie Thibeault, Andrew W. Young, M S W and those
   who donated anonymously.

For providing publishing insights...
   Gerry Birr, John McMahon and Michael Burt, Peace of Mind Bookstore

For determining content...
   Laurie Ouellette, Maggie Wright, Brad Mulhearn, Pat Bourque,
   Thelma Hutton, Gary Eager, Lorraine Bilodeau, Maureen
   Abraham, Katie Stuart, Kathe Tortorice, Melanie Nesheim,
   Kathleen Langone and Lynn Ashworth

For editing...
   Paul Beique and Ed Crouch

For legal matters...
   Steven G. Brown, E S Q., McSwiney, Semple, Bowers & Wise,
   P.C., Concord, N H

For computer systems support...
   Helen, Serge and Cathy Cryvoff, Carol and Steve Furstenau and
   Bill and Kathy Lundgren, OEM Marketing Inc., Auburn, N H

For photography...
   Julie Hamilton (jacket flap), Joe Perrotta, C E O, Portrait Arts
   Photography, Hudson, N H (jacket cover)

For printing, guidance and outstanding customer service...
   Tom Meighan, President, Printed Image Inc., Manchester, N H

For the words and revitalization of the spirit...
   Anna Willis

DICK WILLIS
Publisher / Editor
April 1994

Note from the Author

GOOD STORIES MUST not be explained. Messages they contain are for the recipient alone. We attend to them, feel them and absorb them as if we ourselves have lived them. We hear them in resonance with our unique experience. We instantly recognize their validity and arrive at our next moment profoundly changed.

GOOD STORIES MOVE us along a path of discovery and adventure. If they touch our spirits, it is because they resonate with the ring of truth. In them we find that we are no different from one another; we recognize that we share a common humanity. Their simplicity gives us permission to resume our lives more openly, wisely and with diminished self-deceit.

GOOD STORIES HAVE layers of meaning ready for harvesting. When we ingest them, we are nourished and strengthened for our journey. As we travel, we find others walking with us. Some carry bags laden beyond our own. We speak words of comfort; we share our food; we offer a hand; we laugh and cry together. We hug.

THE ROLE OF PARENT, or child, or aunt, or uncle, or grandparent carries no rule book with it. It is our response to the circumstances of our lives. We each live our own story, and we must tell it. Within its reality lies profound insight and disguised truth. Daring to speak our tale, we can bring new life to those with whom we travel. Our journey can be a blessing or a curse. Love makes the difference.

Contents

Introduction

WITH BREAD and salt, ancient symbols of hospitality and warmth, I welcome you here to share my writings. The greeting I bring comes from a deep tradition established long ago by many peoples and in many lands. My own family roots lie buried in two Eastern European countries.

DAD WAS BORN IN RUSSIA under the czarist regime. Soon after Dad's birth, his father died and his mother raised him carefully with the loving tutelage of her brother-in-law, a Russian Orthodox priest. Dad grew up a horseman, was educated well in a regional military academy and rode with the Don Cossacks in Russia's Bolshevik Revolution.

By age 18 he already had 900 cavalrymen in his command. It was their charge to defend the Russian crown against revolutionaries. The guerrilla war, undertaken to defeat Communism and protect his faith, stretched across the steppes of western Russia.

As a result, he was wounded several times, suffered the ravages of typhus, was nursed back to health by an herbalist-nurse and eventually risked returning home to say farewell to his mother. When he found her, she was slowly dying of starvation because of wartime privations and her stubborn refusal to abandon her home. Her name was Anna.

Despite the horror of the war, Dad's strategic skills in the field confused and, consequently, defeated great numbers of enemy forces. His considerable success resulted in the Communist Party's putting a price on his head.

Fearing for his life, he escaped to Turkey, trained horses for the

British army and ultimately booked passage for America. Having arrived in a land he dreamed would be a place of freedom and dignity, he instead found himself on Ellis Island. Swarming around him was what appeared to be a human cattle drive. Those newly arrived were required to undergo rigorous examination before they were deemed worthy and able to begin life in America.

As one of the newly arrived, Dad was first required to be pronounced physically fit to enter the Home of The Brave. After passing through multiple examinations, he eventually found himself walking alone down a doorless, narrow corridor leading toward still another, unknown procedure.

Noticing that the letters L.L. had been written indelibly on his white shirt just before his newest detour had begun, he struggled to untangle its code. "L.L." ... what could it mean?

"Surely it's important enough for them to send me down this alley alone!" His mind raced.

"Left Leg!" That was it! He had been thrice wounded there, and he limped. Quickly, he removed the shirt, stuffed it into his bag, and practiced walking limpless. There! He could fool them!

As he emerged from the tunnel into a large open orthopedic examining room, Dad met a young doctor obviously waiting to detect his imperfection.

"Walk for me!" he ordered. Dad walked, straight and tall and steady.

"Why did they send you *here*?" the young doctor wondered aloud.

"I don't know," Dad replied innocently.

"I don't, either. You look fine to me. Go ahead through that door, then, and rejoin your buddies," the doctor pronounced. "And good luck in America!" He was grinning.

After a brief try at Henry Ford's assembly line in Detroit, Dad fled in relief back to New York City. There he established his home and became a cabbie. All the boroughs became his terrain as he chauffeured his fares throughout the greater metropolitan network.

MOM WAS BORN to the clear mountain air of southern Poland. Her family owned land, employed many helpers and treasured education for its children. Early memories were filled with gypsy tales, music, hiking, good food and a profoundly rich Catholic tradition.

Her father was wealthy and generous. So generous, in fact, that he agreed to co-sign a note on behalf of a family friend. It was not long before that friend abandoned his payments and disappeared. Mom's father was left having to sell as many of his assets as he could to pay the considerable default. Stopping short of selling his beloved home, he left his family there and set sail for America to earn the remaining sum.

At the time, it was commonly held among Europeans that America was *the* land of opportunity. Quite literally, people believed that streets were lined with gold ready for the picking. What Mom's father found instead were factory sweat shops belching soot and misery. It was in one of these that he secured his employment; soon he was able to send home sufficient money to complete the repayment.

Much to his dismay, however, World War I broke out a short time later. Fearing for his family's safety, he sent them ship's passage for America. Consequently, Mom abandoned her plans to begin normal-school studies in Poland and reluctantly obeyed her father's summons to sail for New York.

Heartbroken over her thwarted plans to get a teaching certificate, Mom quickly realized she needed to work. Money was tight, and she couldn't afford college. So she enrolled in business school, completed her secretarial course and soon began clerking for the Bridgeport Brass Company. There she worked hard ... harder than most because she was the only woman on the production floor.

After several years, she obtained employment at the city health department. There she performed secretarial duties, this time supporting medical professionals attempting to serve countless immigrants unable to understand English. Her bilingual facility was invaluable in diagnosing and treating health problems, in taking clinical histories and in linking families with their missing relatives. She loved it.

The Great Depression had just begun. Everyone was out of work. Mom, however, always managed to have a job. Because her father earned too meager a wage, she felt it appropriate to donate the bulk of her salary to the family coffers. She kept only two dollars a week as her personal allowance. With it, she managed to meet all her remaining needs.

IN THE MEANTIME, Dad had gotten a job making furniture for a wealthy New York manufacturer. He had shown a ready grasp of woodworking and had taken a course in pattern-making to hone his skills.

Mom met Dad at a Russian New Year's Eve dance. She was impressed with the uniformed officer in dress blues; he was charming, gallant and mysterious. He commanded respect and attention from those around him and was the life of the party.

They exchanged telephone numbers, tucked them into their evening clothes and forgot them till the next year. When they met again the following year at the same event, they decided it was right to begin corresponding. They started dating. Good times, good food, good friends … they grew as abundantly as their relationship.

Dad and a close friend were frequent visitors at her parents' home, but Mom knew any thoughts of marriage would meet with vigorous disapproval from her parents. After all, these men were *Russians*! … the people at whose hands Poles had suffered so bitterly throughout their long history. For centuries the Don Cossacks had looted and raped and humiliated them. Marry one? Hardly a palatable thought!

Not until halfway to the ceremony did Mom tell her maid of honor where they were going and why. She and Dad would be married, secretly, in the rectory of a Catholic church in New York. Only the two witnesses would attend. No family.

For an entire year, Mom continued commuting to the City so she could keep any hint of her marriage from her parents. When a friend finally told them, her parents disowned her. Hurt, feeling betrayed, they cut off all contact with her. Mom wrote letter after letter asking for their forgiveness. Ten years passed.

MOM AND DAD BEGAN their married years in New York. Soon, though, Dad was sent to supervise a new manufacturing venture in central New York. His work was admired, and his ability to supervise workers well recognized. They decided to go.

After two years they bought a farm, where they spent the happiest and most hardworking years of their lives. It's where we came into the picture, too.

My brother and I were born a year apart. We were World War II children, raised on a farm, isolated from the culture around us because we spoke only Russian. We worked hard tending to animals, cultivating the garden, harvesting, haying and putting food away.

We were one another's only playmates until we began school. Worried about how we'd adjust not knowing the language, our parents never knew that we secretly listened to radio programs at bedtime. We learned American rapidly and moved effortlessly into our second language.

Meanwhile, through the intervention of a priest, Mom became reconnected with her parents. Arriving for their first visit to the farm, they found themselves wondering which of the two Russians they'd entertained in their home had ultimately married their daughter. They were relieved it was Dad. They liked him.

MOM HAD ALWAYS wanted to be a teacher. She was one. But not in classrooms as she'd expected. She taught us at home, instead ... pouring over school papers, checking notes at the piano bench, preparing food in the kitchen ... always by example. She still teaches us the same way.

At age 86 she attends daily Mass, rides the old bike I bought growing up, gives time to benevolent community activities and maintains her vigorously independent lifestyle.

She has always been keeper of the hearthside. Responsible for instilling values and maintaining the home, she checked homework, typed termpapers, nursed ills and ministered to our growing pains. She stayed home full time but was non-stop busy about all the tasks of keeping a farm, entertaining guests and preparing mountains of hearty food.

That's why Dad felt it was Mom who raised us; but, he was wrong. His spirit – rising animated through every task he undertook, charging through our vigorous after-dinner debates, silently contemplating God's earth in the fields at dusk, gently tendering to animals hurt or calving or caught in barbed wire – animated our lives.

He was a carpenter, a storyteller, a reader, a lover of life. All this bounty and untold more he gave graciously. He was Father.

I remember his funeral in 1968. Endless lines encircled the city block outside the funeral home during visiting hours. The people who came to pay tribute included doctors, lawyers, judges, contractors, laborers and housewives for whom he'd done home repairs. They were old and young, rich and not-so, priests and reporters and politicians. Seldom has that small central New York town seen such an outpouring.

THIS IS MY HERITAGE. Simple and strong.

With no pretense, I bring you with me now to see my world of family. It is a hearth-side vision, perhaps an old-fashioned one flavored with a different time and place.

It is also one profoundly anchored in this new country, America, a more youthful and hopeful one than the heritage from which my parents came. I carry these many traditions in my heart.

And so I welcome you to my home. Make yourselves comfortable. Enjoy the tales I tell. May you find your own startling truths hidden gently inside.

Love and hugs,
ANNA CRYVOFF WILLIS
March 1994
Salem, New Hampshire

Caution:
I Brake for Plastic Bags

Observations of Family

FAMILIES ARE all around us, everywhere we go. We observe them, try to understand, reach out, learn and grow from them. They form our picture of what we are, what we don't want to be. We have to respond; we cannot pass without being affected. Each screams its own message to us.

THE MALL IS BUSY. Mom and dad don't seem very happy. One of the boys says something to his parents. Mom whacks him on the side of his head. Shock waves hit passers-by; they pretend not to notice.

IT'S GRADUATION DAY. One daughter is the valedictorian; her sister, the salutatorian. Their mother has not come to hear them deliver their addresses. "She said she's not into that sort of thing," they excuse. Heartbreak.

A MOTHER STOPS to call home. It's 10:30 P.M. and the board meeting is finally finished. As people prepare to leave, they notice that she has tears in her eyes as she gathers up her papers.

"I haven't seen my little one all day she explains, "She was still asleep when I left at the crack of dawn, and she'll be in bed when I get home. I miss her."

It's her daughter. She quickly decides to take the next day off so she can be with her. Everyone cheers.

A YOUNG WOMAN of 17 stands in her cap and gown before her classmates. She prepares to sing "Wind Beneath My Wings" on behalf of the graduating class when the sound of her crying

2½-year-old rings out, "Mommy!" A young man rises with the little girl and exits; all she knows is that her mom is up there and she wants to be with her, too.

As the song rings out, the crying recedes. From time to time the singer's voice cracks; a soft, male voice can be heard, just barely, lending support when the young woman falters. It's her dad, eyes moist beneath the slicked-down gray of his hair.

THE NEWS SPREAD like wildfire. An 11-year-old, seemingly healthy and planning to play softball in two days, is abruptly diagnosed with lymphoma. He is rushed to a Boston hospital. The diagnosis is confirmed; treatment begins immediately; he lies silent in the intensive care unit.

Families call families, "What can we do to help?" Parents hug their children more tenderly, more often, more spontaneously. They live with the suffering of the stricken child's family. They pray. They hope the prognosis will be good.

MOM IS WORRIED. Her little girl has been observed hitting her head on furniture, on the wall and on doorjambs. She's been whiny and clingy, it seems, over the past few weeks. What's wrong? What should she do?

There's a reason her behavior has changed recently: A new baby has come on the scene. She has been feeling cast out, passed over, less loved, not important. How come mommy is stressed and irritable? She just doesn't understand.

After sharing with another mom, this young woman suddenly gets the picture. She turns her love toward the little girl's pain: "I love you, honey!", hugs, time alone just doing what they've always enjoyed doing together, sharing the baby's good times; helping one another to comfort, hold, feed, change the new baby; moving into a gently transforming relationship.

One morning mom hears, "I love you, Mommy!" Things are better. Much.

EVERYONE'S EXCITED. Birthdays are a big deal for this family. Brother is coming home to celebrate … cards, gifts, special foods, a chocolate birthday cake with icing messages carefully composed. Calls seem to be coming in from everywhere. Strains of "Happy Birthday to You …" can be heard long distance from those unable to come for the party.

But Dad can't come as first planned; he's been called to work; there's been trouble and he must see it through. Unexpected guests and family gather watching as faces drop and spirits deflate. "It'll be OK," someone mutters, "we'll party again tomorrow!" Being together means everything.

FAMILY. It's the center of our most caring selves. It has many colors and textures. It stirs deep emotions, generates great tenderness and provokes painful isolation in the midst of the belonging. It's where we come from; it's what we want to become. It's the food of our endless meditations.

Trust Your Gut

"**T**RUST YOUR GUT." I heard the care in my friend's voice. A dilemma had just arisen in my life, and I didn't know what to do. I hoped for a word of wisdom from him, and he was telling me that I held the answer deep within.

My friend was intent on encouraging me. He had some years of psychological practice under his belt, and I looked up to the knowledge and experience he carried.

"He's just being nice to me," I thought as I heard him. How do I go about trusting that quiet little voice speaking deep inside? What if I'm crazy and naive and wrong in my assessment of what's going on here? There's too much at stake. I might damage a perfectly innocuous situation and blow everything. Then what?

Feeling as though I was jumping off a cliff, I decided to do as he suggested. I tensed, stepped out, fell into the abyss, and felt the yank as my parachute opened. To my surprise, I felt myself floating gently to the ground and whispered a prayer of thanks as my feet touched down.

"Trust your gut!" I've since passed his advice on to those I've met who have found themselves in quandary ... agonized, struggling against badly fitted advice, seeking to love those whom their actions affect.

And maybe that's the criterion against which we must measure the validity of our "gut": Is our heart engaged in a shouting match with our head over the choice of our action?

SEVERAL YEARS AGO my husband became quite ill. Feeling he needed hospital attention, I brought him there. He received a diagnosis that seemed plausible and was discharged with medication. My gut, though, told me something was wrong. Waiting the whole day, uncertain, I couldn't quiet my little voice. Finally, deciding to seek a second opinion, I drove him to another hospital. There, my husband underwent a second examination. Not surprisingly, it revealed an entirely different diagnosis.

It was agreed that he required immediate emergency surgery. Several agonizing hours later, we were approached by the surgeon who had performed the operation. He revealed that, had we waited till morning, my husband's life would have been lost. We had gotten him there just in the nick of time. My gut was right.

As the mother of three teens, I frequently relied on my gut to help decide the wisdom of giving various permissions.

Asking if she could take in a day of skiing with friends, my daughter detailed her plans for the trip and awaited my OK. Something gray and nebulous nagged at me as she spoke.

"What's my big problem here?" I listened to my internal dialogue. "Why doesn't this feel right? I know the kids with whom she's traveling, I know the driver, I know where they'll be. They're just going for the day. Why am I holding back my permission?"

When she approached me for my final decision the next day, she understandably expected my go-ahead. Instead, I confessed my hesitancy and, in my intentional vagueness, tossed the ultimate decision back onto her shoulders.

I still remember seeing her face studying me. "What do you see, Mom?" she inquired, mystified.

"No more than an indistinct haze, a gray color," I answered.

She became thoughtful and then made her decision. She wouldn't go with them.

The day of her friends' trip dawned sunny and bright. It would be a wonderful skiing day! My guilt over the role I'd played in her refusal to go grew as the day passed. What sort of weirdo was I that I had stood in the way of some good fun with friends?

It was not until the following day that we heard the news. The carfull had never reached its destination. During the first half-hour of their trip the passengers experienced engine trouble. Between hiking for help, getting towed, bickering with unfamiliar garage mechanics and arranging transportation home laden with ski gear, the young travelers had endured a miserable day.

"Thanks, Mom," my daughter came with the news. "You knew something, didn't you?"

"Was anyone hurt?" I avoided a direct answer.

"No, but their trip was shot!" She walked slowly away, shaking her head.

PEOPLE HAVE SHARED countless stories such as these with me. Moms have told of the urgings they've gotten when a child has been sick or troubled, even if miles away. Parents have spoken of their compulsions to send their son a check, to call Grandma, to drop unexpectedly by the home of a friend they've not seen in months.

Considerable study has attended the puzzling phenomenon described here. What it all eventually boils down to, though, is that we seem to have a faculty beyond our usual conscious and rational one, one that operates between us and those we love. Mysterious though it may be, I am convinced it's real and important and urgent.

Whatever obstacles we create in acting on our gut feelings are of our own making: They usually hinge on our stubborn insistence that behavior must make sense. If it doesn't, we tell ourselves we must be crazy. But maybe "crazy" isn't so bad? Maybe trusting our gut is a gift we need to nurture and embrace as part of our own wonderfully spiritual nature.

Ode to Mothers

LAST NIGHT I visited a childbirth class. Stretched out on mats were the expectant mothers and their coaches listening intently to the experienced instructor. She was telling how to pack the hospital suitcase and where to hang the homecoming clothes so that everything would be ready. "Plan to wear your 6th-month pregnancy clothes home," she warned.

I could almost hear the hearts hit bottom: "You mean I won't be back to my size 8?" No wonder mom's self-esteem erodes so predictably as delivery nears!

Think about it. Mom never knows what size clothing to pull off the rack; she pops in the borrowed Jane Fonda exercise tape and, bending over for her first morning stretch, hears the insistent cry from the nursery; after she puts the baby down to sleep, she rushes around vacuuming, dusting and ironing so she can face the house with a bit more equanimity. And now her own time is being stolen by the little monkey! Looks like she lost *that* round!

More than one mother I've met has bragged that her proudest maternal accomplishment was finally having picked up all the Legos.

Whatever happened to the romantic picture of the fulfilled woman, the happy homemaker, the ever-patient caretaker of her young? Did she take a wrong turn somewhere? Did she misplace her good sense of self somewhere in the laundry hamper? Does she feel incompetent, listless, frumpy, alien like an amoeboid inhabitant of some nether world to which she was sold a one-way ticket? Is she lost in the frantic shuffle otherwise known as the blissful state of motherhood?

Let's take a look at what we know about self-esteem. It's based on our accomplishments and on our credible acknowledgment by others. It also helps if our accomplishments are concrete, so we can touch and feel and admire them. All those who work in service-oriented fields know about burnout and what's needed to repair it. But moms don't. When they're burned out, they think it's some deficiency within themselves; the magazines tell them they should be happy and able to make their own clothes and curtains and keep spotless houses and well-dressed, smiling babies.

But reality looks more like this: Meals take three hours to prepare and 15 minutes to devour; dust collects in two hours, just in time for the arrival of company; punctuality is forever lost as mom bends over one last time to pick up roller skates left on the stair; conversations reduce to one-syllabled, telegraphic utterances; well-laid plans get abruptly changed when Emily breaks out in those funny-looking red spots; mom's right ear subjected to long years of car pooling no longer even registers sound vibrations. The litany goes on and on.

And yet she rocks the cradle and kisses the hurts; she quiets the nightmares and oversees the school projects and goes to PTA meetings and runs the scout troop and cries when children leave, one by one. All hail to Mom! She's the stuff of heroes.

BUT, HOLD IT! Mom's becoming all empty inside. She needs some small measure of self- confidence restored, some good feelings about herself rekindled, some dignity back. Is this unthinkable, or can it be done? Let's take a look.

Mom needs first to take some time for adult friendships – with no kids around. She should be given the opportunity to spend one hour a week, minimum, outside the house and engaged in fascinating conversation with someone she enjoys who has reached at least her 20TH birthday and appears relatively sane.

She next needs to realize that motherhood is not a competitive indoor sport. Rather than comparing her children's developmental milestones with others in an effort to establish her own superiority in the mothering role, mom instead should support and cooperate with other moms. Ever been to one of those awful holding tank waiting areas where moms gather to pick up their young? If it's not a bitching session or a one-upmanship duel, it's a marathon recipe-exchange.

Some bragging is tolerable, but most of the time moms should join forces to help one another get a leg up: having a room painting or papering day while a paid sitter watches the kids; setting up babysitting exchanges to give one another an hour's brake a week to shop blissfully alone or get a badly needed haircut or a green mud facial.

Picking a project that can get done in an hour and displayed on the front door or on a wall or window can really help the self-esteem. Then, by insisting that kids go to their rooms for a "quiet time" right after lunch, mom can take the time to fix herself a cup of tea and sit down with the latest hot novel. An entire hour a day … think of it! It could be a domestic revolution! It *can* be done if mothers of the world unite to restore "alone time" to some small portion of their otherwise selfless day.

And what if moms start their day with a shower before kids get up, followed by a cup of steaming, aromatic coffee, a bagel or muffin or full-grained toast?

And, say! What if they greet that sleep-deprived, every-hair-out-of-place reflection in the bathroom mirror at 6 a.m. with, "You're OK, Kid! I like your style!" Being weird or crazy or unpredictable at least once a day helps sanity a lot.

If moms take a moment each day, a *right-now*, don't-wait-till-tomorrow moment in which they give themselves permission to restore their own peculiar kind of peace, they'll discover how truly wonderful they are.

To Fathers

WHAT UNMITIGATED GALL, writing about fathers when I'm not one! How can a mother speak of what she has not known? Why, even?

Because I need to tell dads how critical they are to their children's development – and to the lives of the women they love.

FIRST, THOUGH, I must issue my own disclaimer: Family circumstances often dictate the roles played by its members. Traditional expectations get re-examined when economic and cultural conditions change. Mothers and fathers search their souls and do what they must do to sustain the family's life. Together, they build their brand new relationships and learn to operate in tenuous times. If their solutions bear no resemblance to what they expected when they first married, they battle their discomforts and travel the untried road they've chosen. This takes phenomenal courage, strength and hard work.

DADS ARE PIVOTAL to the healthy growth of their children. Dr. T. Berry Brazelton describes the behavior of father-deprived infants studied at Boston Children's Hospital as starving for male touch and vocalization.

"They're saying, 'Mom is not enough,' even at these early times in life," he laments.

Other researchers have claimed that daughters growing up without a male in their lives are unable to resolve their emerging sexuality in adolescence. This leaves them with two postures with which to form future love relationships with men: either hating or fearing them.

The traditional male role involves dad as the bread winner. If the family culture maintains this posture, dad's perspective is a marketplace one. He sees the global view of decisions made within the household, the macro-picture. This lends the nature of family direction an authority valid for the long term. It's a perspective that a mother who has chosen to stay home doesn't have. She's looking closer to the home, neighborhood, school and township view.

If it's a business experience he brings home, dad adds a future orientation, a bottom-line profit/loss disposition to family fiscal matters.

Dads who shoulder the burden of bread winner make sure the family's basic needs can be met. The load is frequently a heavy one. It is assumed by dad simply because that's what the world expects of him. He's been raised that way. When for reasons of unemployment or underemployment he is unable to fulfill it, he is overwhelmed by it.

Perhaps the best comfort we can give is to grant dads permission to share their self-doubts and disappointments.

Yes, most women would much rather lean on a pillar of strength than shoulder life and parenthood alone. But dads don't have to build and maintain that pillar all by themselves. They need to remember that they've got helpmates.

Those helpmates want dads to know that it's OK to be vulnerable. Sharing burdens is the right of spouses. Allowing feelings to surface so they can be talked through with a loving partner is the stuff of a growing couple. It's not a sign of weakness. Quite the contrary, most women consider it a courageous act.

Regardless whether dads find themselves at home or in the work place, though, they lend a unique perspective to family function and child-rearing. Men and women think differently. Those differences present a wholeness to the process that cannot be duplicated by a single parent, no matter how complete or conscientious or dedicated.

Dads have always brought a special physical gift to their children. I'm completely aware of many moms who enjoy vigorous activity, but the particular physicalness of dads seems different. Observational studies of moms and dads playing with their young seem to suggest that dads roughhouse, toss, wrestle with, and handle children with more gusto than moms do. This type of play gives the young a more daring experience, a more thrill-engendering one than mom's gentle touch.

Researchers regularly speak of father bonding as being as critical as the mother's. Babies respond quite differently to dads than to moms: active excitement vs. quiet gurgling.

Clearly a balance in children's play can only happen when both parents undertake it. Dad's absence or rare presence results in their missing out.

Dads, by their actions and attitudes, teach children how to treat moms. When parents are in hostile combat, the children reflect the father's posture. If he puts her down, so do they. But if dad is tender and loving, the children follow suit, making sure they are respectful and gentle.

The wonder of this phenomenon rests in dad's power. I marvel that his voice, deeper and more commanding, gets children's attention over mom's. Despite the wide range of male personality types, dad's authority still seems to speak more loudly.

There seems little doubt about it. Children look up to dad to steer the family ship. What magic makes this happen I don't know.

"Mom made the decisions in the family," confessed one young man. "But we always sought out dad. It wasn't until he reiterated her decision that things started happening."

Families need the partnership of both parents. Dads must defer to moms when appropriate; moms should reciprocate in kind. Complementary roles make the whole business of raising a family possible. One is not better or smarter or wiser or gentler just because of sex. We mysteriously choose spouses who have gifts we ourselves lack. We're not the same, nor should we be. But honor one another we must.

MY DAD WAS a traditional father. He worked hard, brought home the money and gave the last word on family decisions. But he felt a significant piece of his life was missing, as the following story shows.

One night he and I were driving home from an important scholarship interview at the college I was later to attend. He'd had a drink with friends and was feeling sentimental, even to the point of asking me to drive the seven hours back home.

"Your mother raised you with no help from me," he confessed. "All I did was bring in the money."

My shock at his blindness was covered by the darkness in which we rode.

"Don't you know how profoundly you fathered me?" I cried. "You brought me your culture, your strength, your passion for life, your discipline and unspoken love. You have been the anchor, the rock from which I go confidently into my new life. How can you ever question the depth of your presence to me?"

I heard him quietly crying beside me.

He died in 1968, and with him my God. It wasn't until ten years later that I began coming to terms with the "God-father" connection. I wept then and allowed my belated mourning to erupt. It was then that I admitted my rage at his abandonment through death. I started attending church once more. I could again speak the "Our Father" beyond "Thy kingdom come ...."

Fathers, we honor you. We raise the flag of your quiet giving. We invite you to drink deeper of our family's life.

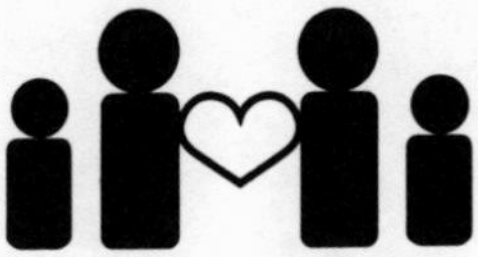

On Loving Children

"WHAT CHILDREN NEED most in life is to feel loved by their parents." Lillian Katz, nationally known child development specialist, shared these thoughts with us at a New Hampshire Early Childhood meeting some years ago. I never forgot what she said.

Most parents truly love their children, yet countless youngsters never get the message. They see their parents' love as conditional: It is given only when behavior is suitable, when they have achieved a notable goal, when they dress well, when they bring home scholastic honors. So they spend their waking hours trying to please parents. Without parental love, children feel inadequate, useless, bad.

If it's so important to children that they feel loved, how can parents make sure that their love message gets through? Since kids are so good at sniffing out the real from a field of counterfeit messages, parents must work at sending consistent and genuine vibes that they do truly and unconditionally love the children.

First, let's look at how children view the messages they believe. They know that words alone can't be trusted; adults break promises, expect behavior of others that they themselves don't follow, change moods at will and expect children to shift their actions accordingly.

In a nutshell, children know that what we do is what we really mean. By the time they reach adolescence, they have finally gotten up the guts to challenge our inconsistencies with utterances like, "Words are cheap!" And they're absolutely right!

Next, we must know that children zero in on those in their lives who are constant and predictable. Sounds boring, doesn't it?

Not if you're young and vulnerable to the whims of older folk with god-like authority over you. It's scary when you don't have a clue what this parent is going to do next. If you hit sister before breakfast and mom doesn't flinch but hitting her just before dinnertime brings an outrageous punishment, you've got a predictability problem. Children need to know that parents have behavioral rules that, when violated, always produce the same response.

Another clear communication easily understood by children is this one: "I'll love you no matter what you have done. You're entitled to make mistakes. Most mistakes can be fixed. I'm here to help you learn from them and grow."

Mistakes don't necessarily indicate a character flaw. They usually mean the doer had a bout of shortsightedness. If parents assume that most children try to do their best most of the time, they can extend this same disposition to their children.

The result of giving children this benefit-of-the-doubt is long-range: They'll be assured of continued understanding and support. They'll know their parents believe in their intrinsic worth as people. They'll know that, come mistakes or successes, the significant adults in their lives will be there for them.

"You were always there when I needed you!"– the finest words a child can speak to a parent.

Do gentleness and warmth communicate as signs of love? Some parents are reluctant to give these, and children sometimes resist receiving them. They recognize these gestures, though, as the face of love.

Timing is vital when parents deliver these kinds of signals. Adults must have a clear fix on which types of situations could be helped with gentleness. They need to apply spontaneity and genuineness in the use of them – a touch, a hug, an understanding smile, a gentle nudge, a wink. Loving gestures can come by surprise. They can burst forth in the midst of company or family or strangers. They can speak clearly of parental pride and affection.

Tenderness speaks volumes of parental love, too. I often see mothers or fathers pulling children along the street as if they were inanimate, or spanking them in the grocery aisle, or brushing their hair so roughly it brings tears.

Gentleness means taking care to treasure the physical self of children. It communicates tenderness. It teaches children that their bodies are sacred, precious and worthy of care-filled treatment. It settles deeply into their expectations for future loving relationships and sets the stage for their personal growth.

"But, wait!" you say. "Is the face of love always gentle and warm and saccharine? Must adults always look like sugarcoated candy bars to their kids?" Not really. Sometimes parents should be firm, should expect difficult things, should set inconvenient but wise rules. Children know that parental admonitions speak love as surely as parental softness.

Young adults have frequently told me that they know parents love them by setting and enforcing curfews, by insisting that they repair damage done, by repaying loans, by keeping promises despite personal inconvenience.

Why? Because, in the midst of living out day-to-day confusions, children recognize and respond to parental respect. They know when adults listen. They recognize fair and equitable parental treatment.

Caring means respecting; respect lives in our actions. It transmits strength and openness and affirmation. It listens with the heart and ears. It honors the tenderness of the spirit and seeks never to hurt. It is honest and unyielding and committed.

Love seeks to follow through on what is demanded. It recognizes how easy it is to say, "Don't do that," and no more. Parents must first catch the violation, then correct it and set it right. "Be home at 10," is only step one. Step two means that someone must stay awake to greet the homecomer.

A mother recently told me that her son accused her of no longer caring about him. Why? Because she had said nothing about the pile of dirty clothes on his bedroom floor. Normally, she would have brought it to his attention but this time ignored it.

Follow through! Children know it means that parents love them. They know how much energy it takes to attend to the details of their lives while simultaneously attending to our own.

Children know that time is love, too. Taking precious moments just for them is a kindness they recognize. A dear friend makes sure each afternoon that she meets her daughters at the bus and sits them down for a tea party together.

Yesterday, my littlest one tried to share a new idea with me; he saw that I was preoccupied, and gently prodded, "Mom, you've gone away!" I quickly returned. "Pay attention," I chided myself. "You'll get invited more often into his thoughts and dreams."

Do the unexpected! They'll know it's love. Surprise them with a Saturday morning breakfast at a favorite diner; take them for a walk ... the world is all around. Parents and children need to share it.

Caring enough to confront presents yet another face of love. Constructive confrontation targets behavior, not personal worth. It's rooted in a profound respect for the person being confronted. It leaves room for response and explanation. It assures the confronter's readiness to listen. It holds both self and "other" responsible for action. It takes love and guts.

"Doing for" is *not* loving our children. It's a lazy thing to do. Children know this well but try to get others to serve them, nevertheless. If they're to grow in competence, though, they must learn to try, to struggle, to participate, to help out. Teaching them what we know and encouraging them in their somewhat awkward efforts shows them *real* love.

Love them with courage and gentleness and energy. Your love is life-giving.

Power Plays

"She just wouldn't put on the clothes I'd bought for her school pictures!" snapped a distraught mother who'd sent her child off to school in tears, after what most of us would recognize as a full-blown power play. Why won't our children do it our way? Why can't they bow to our infinite wisdom and be more like us?

At the heart of a Power Play is the child's insistence that she wants to try it her way. A physician told me he'd fought hard to earn the right to make his own mistakes and considered this one of the best gifts he could pass on to his son! In a book I've been reading, the author speaks of trial-and-error as being a lost art; trial-and-rightness is how we're raised, he noted, and we've become the poorer for it. Why are we so afraid of making mistakes, and, more critically, of allowing our children learn from making their mistakes, too?

In the parent-child tug of war (the Power Play) there's something important going on. Children need to lead as well as be led. When our fourth was born into a family of three teens and two adults, he also came under the scrutiny of five supervisors. How can anyone work under those circumstances, much less live there? Our adolescents were feeling the need to raise a perfect brother despite anything Ben had to say about the matter! So, they told him what to do, when to do it, how, and whether or not he'd succeed. (By their standards!) Being the wonderful child he is, Ben made his declaration of independence early, and the power plays began.

So, how do we handle these horrible things? Aren't strong-minded people also powerful and well able to live competent lives, often making a great difference in their societies? Indeed! But living with the strong-willed person is difficult; our job as parents is to harness this energy so that it leads to a creative, productive, flexible adulthood. It must not become destructive or vindictive.

There are some basic strategies we can implement so that this determination to "do it my way" can work for the child's growth rather than for his/her ultimate discouragement.

RULE 1 : Know when you're in a Power Play. You'll feel frustrated and angry and want to throw a tantrum. "How can this child be so obstinate?!" you'll hear yourself say. But seldom will you recognize that you're being equally bullheaded.

RULE 2 : Step back about 15 paces and say to yourself, "Golly, here comes a power play now!" This pulling back will give you a chance to get a bit of perspective, and, chances are, will produce more positive effects than *re*-acting impulsively.

RULE 3 : Recognize that your child has thoughts and feelings, too. Voice yours, but not with anger; then invite her to do the same. If you find yourself furious, retreat into the bathroom until you calm down. Tell your youngster you'll be back soon. Self-regulation like this is great modeling! Use it. Once the feelings and opinions are out, you'll at least know where each of you is coming from.

RULE 4 : Give choices, compromise, negotiate, problem-solve, brainstorm: show your willingness to be flexible and creative.

You know what works really well? A sense of the ridiculous. This disarms the power struggle and gets everybody laughing – something we don't do nearly enough! We sometimes take this job of winning at parenting far too seriously. Lighten up!

RULE 5 : If your child entrenches and decides to do "none of the above," do the unexpected. One mom, when her son kept forgetting to feed the cats before dinner (a passive Power Play), "forgot" to fill his plate as she had those of other family members. He caught on in a flash, grinned in appreciation of her humor, fed the critters and never neglected his job again. No emotion, no nagging or criticism; just an action response calling forth a challenge to see the situation differently. It works, but you risk being playful or creative or innovative. Dare to change your own rules once in awhile.

RULE 6: Choose your battles wisely. If you're constantly finding yourself in power struggles with your child, it's time for a cease-fire. Retreat and ask yourself if you need always to be in control. "It's a lot easier," admitted one parent, "to just have it my way all the time." When she heard what she'd said, she suddenly came up short. Is that what she'd really wanted?

When we're in a hurry or under pressure, we're most vulnerable to Power Plays. Take a minute to stop, see who's there, realize that we love them a whole lot and ask for a group hug. "I need your cooperation if we're going to make it," might work really well.

Which battles should we fight? The important ones. Like no liquor at teen parties; no playing near the road; always telling family where you'll be and when you're returning. When it's a matter of safety or good judgment or the physical or moral law, stand on your own firm ground. Don't move. You must be the wall against which your children can bounce in order to learn some of life's most important lessons.

When do we *not* compromise or negotiate or give choices? When children are hurting themselves, others, or property – three immovable laws that should be enforced at all costs. They are rooted in honor and respect, they produce responsible and competent people.

Five-year-old Ben was outside riding his bike dressed only in shirtsleeves. It was cold and windy. I stuck my head out the door and asked if he wanted his jacket. "I'm OK, Mom," he shouted back. A friend was watching and asked whether I was concerned he'd catch cold. "Colds don't come from being cold," I answered. Just then, Ben popped in, grabbed his jacket, and, with a wave and a grin, ran out to resume his play. Whew! One more power struggle avoided. Maybe he'll think of it himself next time!

Understanding

CHILDREN THINK we adults talk too much. It's probably true. Somehow we grown-ups have gotten the message, perhaps from the generation before ours, that we should pass our wisdom onto the younger generation by talking them to death at every available opportunity.

If we look more closely at our own early years, we will undoubtedly remember how we groaned when our elders began expounding on some principle they thought applied in the situation we were facing. We resented their intrusions, felt unheard and, most likely, "turned off" the rest of their lectures.

In a teen group with which I recently spent some time, I saw the adult-youngster roadblock still alive today. One of the teens drew a card from the deck of a game we were playing. It read, "Tell about an understanding person in your life." Dropping her head, the young woman quietly answered, "I don't think I have one. Everybody has something to say, and nobody listens."

She equated understanding with "silent listening," that skill which comes from a heart filled with the wisdom of human nature, with an insightfulness about when and when not to speak. It's that wonderful quality of true friendship that doesn't need to "fix" anything. Instead, it accepts, reaches out in strength and communicates that the hurting person is not alone. It also trusts that the troubled individual will resolve the problem appropriately by themselves and when the time is right.

How strange it is that we feel compelled to have all the answers when youngsters come to us with a care, a hurt, or an insult they've received. Have we not learned, painfully, that our answers don't always work for others? Come to think of it, how often do our answers work for *us*? Why do we think that we can determine the right "fit" for someone else's difficulty? Don't others, in fact, know better than we what they can pull off as a plausible solution?

But we want to help. We care about the young people who have sought us out. How will we assist them without violating their power to choose and implement a personally-tailored solution?

First, we look at who we are: adults who have lived more years than the young; grown- ups who have, presumably, an increased capacity to understand greater numbers of possibilities than they. We frequently have more insight into the meaning of circumstances they've encountered. We see more varieties of choices and more problem junctures. We also grasp more consequences of choices. Like a book, we contain volumes of information that, because of our caring, we can make honestly and openly available to the young person we seek to help.

Comfortable in the knowledge which we've accumulated during our lifetimes, we can listen in silence to the outpourings of their young spirits. We don't jump in with pronouncements, solutions or advice. The only time we speak should be to seek further clarification, to comment or question our grasp of their story. This is the hardest part. An invisible piece of duct tape over the mouth works best to insure success during this stage.

Carefully, we then ask, "What do you think you'll do next?" If this precipitates a flood of emotion, we don't pursue this line of inquiry. It means we haven't yet completed the previous work.

If, on the other hand, they begin thoughtfully considering their options, we've successfully passed over with them into problem-solving mode. This is our chance to throw in their other options, helping them realize that, at any given moment, many different choices are open to them. There is seldom just one. Exploring the field with someone we love can be most helpful and also rewarding.

Next, we investigate where each choice leads. Our assistance here is real. Since our book is chock full of observations and experiences, we can offer this information to help them project the outcome of a particular course of action. This help could influence their decision.

Executing choices, though, is their job, not ours. So are the consequences. If they carry out our solutions, they can also blame us for the results. And ... they will have learned nothing about decision-making or problem-solving. They must own not only their feelings but also their discovery of options. They must feel that their judgments have improved and their repertoire of workable solutions has expanded.

That's how we help them. Not by talking "at" them, not by preaching, not by giving them the answers. These they "read" as a lack in our understanding of them. Instead, we must *listen*. We must ask them to tell us who they are, how they react to the actions of others, what they think is a proper course of response, and how we can be of help to them. Our job is to enlighten their self-knowledge and their knowledge of the world.

We are their teachers and mentors, their cheering sections, their advocates. Trust them to solve their problems well when in the caring company of one who understands them by listening well.

Fantasy: Its Role in Childrearing

"I DON'T WANT my child growing up with unreality, with stories that need to be undone later on." He was worried, this young dad, that the trust he had worked so hard to build with his young child would ultimately be shattered when the youngster found out "the truth."

"Does that mean you'll have no Santa Claus or Easter Bunny or Tooth Fairy?" I gently inquired.

"Well, Santa Claus is alright. After all, he really did live once." He seemed a bit more definite.

"But it's *you* who gives on Santa's behalf," I returned. "And that's real."

What is the role of fantasy, magical traditions and storytelling in the lives of our children? Do these tales damage or enhance? Are they just an indulgence, a way to spoil our children or to keep them in line until that fateful day when our ruse is found out, and our young ones come crashing down with the burden of our deceit?

Myths play a vital role in development. Since recorded history, humankind has felt the need to rise above the ordinary and difficult conditions of life. Our nature seems to require the presence of hope to stay productive, creative and nurturing. So we make up stories based on a reality that our spirits seek to acknowledge but that our eyes fail to see.

These tales reflect our basic humanity with all its glory and vulnerability: We weave stories of cruelty which reflect how we treat one another; we cheer the hero who overcomes impossible odds; we selflessly distribute our wealth to the poor through our mythology; we tremble with those who face the same fears we ourselves know too well; we rehearse situations yet untried, ones we dread, to see how we might conquer them; we transform the drab "everyday" into a new vision ... all through our daily exercise of fantasy.

It's pivotal to our good mental health. To dream, to see things as they might be, to rehearse impending reality so we can dare to risk, to acknowledge that our nature has its own predictable twists and quirks, to ultimately accept one another as we are— these are all fruits of this wonderful gift we call fantasy.

And there's more. It's through the living out of our magical traditions that we learn how to be more gently human.

"I always overdo the basket thing at Easter," confessed a young mom. "And my mother did, too. For her it was an opportunity to over-give, to tip the balance in the direction of generosity." Hurray! Who's to say that's bad? Not I, no ma'am!

Most of us have known times of deep sadness or trouble when we've been unable to get ourselves "up" for a holiday. Deciding to partake in holiday fantasy traditions can sometimes help us get through "down" periods in spite of our melancholy.

My brother served in Vietnam for several years. The first Christmas, Dad in his agony refused to even consider trudging out to the back woods for our yearly tree-cutting. Arriving home from college to his gloom, I decided that Christmas 1965 would look like all the others. We'd do it right despite his suffering; maybe going through the motions would prompt his spirits to rise and restore some peace to our holidays. Christmas had always been a season that held great meaning for our family.

My scheme worked. By the time Christmas Eve rolled around, we had together adorned a particularly beautiful tree, baked and decorated mounds of cookies, delivered boxes filled with them to a pediatric hospital ward nearby, joined in a festive carol sing, and quietly sank into the solemnity of our church's midnight Mass.

"Is Santa real?" the children have asked, each in turn.

We've always said, "Yes" because he's as real as the magic of the love we bear our children. And that's as real as this moment—maybe more so!

Stories, myths, magical traditions are not just childish frivolity. They inspire the growth of imagination, they teach moral lessons as few sermons do, they transform life as we experience it into fresh possibilities, they generate hope, they tell us who we are and what we might become, they speak to our spiritual dimension and urge it to create what has never before been thought. They bring joy and encourage altruism and tell us how to reconcile with one another.

And they give us permission over and over again to be young with our children. Reliving each year with the stories of our heritage brings healing to our own hurt spirits, infusing them with new strength and courage to continue doing our best. It's life lessons we teach when we bring these seemingly trivial celebrations and tales into their young lives; it's not unreality. Indeed, it may be at the very core of reality. Enjoy.

On Self-Esteem

TALKING ABOUT self-esteem is tricky. Its importance is not in dispute, but its meaning seems to slide away from us whenever we try to pin it down; it is somewhere between arrogance and wimpishness.

Self-esteem is almost easier to talk about when we witness the lack of it. In the classroom, it's the lack of confidence to ask a legitimate question, believing it to be stupid. It's not trusting your gut in a particular situation you later learn was exactly what your perceptions told you. It's a sinking feeling that you're not worthy, somehow, of being where you are.

How do we know when our self-esteem is securely in place? It's when we have the assurance that we are important in the scheme of things, that we have something of value to contribute to an effort, that we can make valid decisions and take good risks. Self-esteem is knowing who we are in a very real way, not overestimating or underestimating, but cherishing.

Most of the time, especially when we're doing the most profound growing, we are somewhere between having self-esteem and not having it. As we encounter feedback from others, we must adjust who it is we think we are with what someone else tells us we are. I always think I'm thinner when I enter the doctor's office than I do when I step on that awful scale! My self-esteem always seems to get a blow at the scales; it calls me to accept the new data, and I only care about rejecting it! Sturdy self-esteem ultimately challenges me to admit and incorporate it into my picture of self–or work to change it. In either case, though, I can't turn my back on it. It's who I really am.

So, when thrown a curve ball, we must listen, evaluate and

respond. Our self-esteem, when damaged, must be attended to. We must learn to pull back, take an honest look, face the possibility of having to change something about ourselves and reaffirm that we're worth the herculean effort.

Psychologist Carl Rogers tells us that we as parents play a critical role in laying the foundations of self-esteem in our children. Without a highly developed sense of self, the child must rely on those most important to him or her for healthy self-esteem. Erik Erikson found that, unless the parent creates a trusting and safe environment for the child, the youngster never learns to trust him/herself as a confident person.

Parents are important to their children's belief in themselves. Our actions and attitudes are closely watched and absorbed by our children and become the well from which they draw their sense of self. Here's a brief checklist against which to measure our esteem-building skills as parents:

- Do we *delight* in their presence, not all the time, but enough so they know how precious they are to our lives?
- Do we notice the responsible or considerate things they do, or do we just land on them when they do something wrong?
- Do we speak to their actions, or do we call them "bad" or "selfish" or "inconsiderate" or "sloppy"? If we label the action and not the doer we save the self-esteem.
- Do we give them choices and allow them to make mistakes, or do we try controlling them so they'll be perfect?
- Do we really *listen*, not just for the details, but also for the feelings? Do we accept these feelings and, consequently, validate our children?
- Do we do unexpected, little things that show how much we think about them and love them?
- Do we give them realistic feedback when they come to us with a dilemma? Or, do we tell them what they want to hear so they'll like us better?
- Do we encourage them to try new things on their own? Are we

about the business of encouraging independence and risk-taking in our children, or do we want to hang onto them into old age?
- Do we forgive them or do we lock children into their past offenses, making checklists and reminding them at every opportunity?
- Do we spend time with them so we can build memories to treasure?
- Do we seek through our shared times together to discover who they are and what gifts they have brought into our lives? Children translate our time investment as real value; they feel honored.
- Do we nurture, hug, soothe, comfort, empathize?

And what about us? Do we honor ourselves as we seek to honor our children? Do we pat ourselves on the back and declare in joy, "Atta parent! You've done your work well today!"

About Rules

I KNEW A FAMILY once that lost its foster child because of rules. When the youngster arrived at this family's home, he was given a listing of the few rules by which family members understood they lived out their lives together. But it was the ones they never knew they had that killed their relationship with the young guest before it ever began.

One rule specified that whoever got up first let out the dog. The poor young visitor was never told, and the entire household became furious. Despite his only having been with them for a few days, they judged him inconsiderate and unhelpful. He, on the other hand, found them arbitrary and confusing. The match was soon found inappropriate by the social worker, and the youngster was moved elsewhere.

Needless to say, we must have rules to maintain order. We know our children should grow up knowing that rules are important and must be followed if we're to live together. But what happens when there are too many rules? When do they get in the way of encouraging creative, resourceful people? And when do our rules create defiance because we haven't given our youngsters the opportunity to assert their uniqueness apart from ours? If everything's got to be done according to our directives and methodologies, we imply that deviations must be wrong, and so are they.

Let's make some rules about rule-making, OK? I'll try to make them few and important. In turn, I ask that we all examine whether or not the rules we have created in our families are useful and growth-producing—for adult and child alike.

RULE I: When establishing rules, make sure they're always

right and not relative or arbitrary or based on someone's inclination to adhere to them. Here are three that can always be valid: Thou shalt not hurt yourself, others, or property. Another rule we have in our homes is that, whenever you leave home, you must notify others where you've gone and when you plan to return. These hold true regardless of age or position. Otherwise, there will be worry, concern and ultimate confrontation by those not notified.

The rationale behind all of the rules is the same: We are a caring, responsible community of persons in relationship with one another. Unless we show this by respecting one another and showing our concern for each another, our community breaks down and trust is destroyed. Mutual respect and trust lie at the core of family and must be sustained.

RULE 2: Anyone can make rules, but all must buy into them if they are to be valid. This means that we parents cannot make rules that just apply to the children. If the children must pick up after themselves, so must we. If they must not lie, we can't tell them to say we are not home when Aunt Molly calls. If they must not smoke, neither can we. If they can't cheat, neither can we pad our expense accounts. If they must obey driving laws, we must not go 75 in a 55 zone. Our actions often catch us breaking the very laws we have so strenuously legislated onto our children. They are watching what we do. We must be good models for them.

RULE 3: Watch the "Catch 22" setup! "Your homework comes first," but, "Can't you get a job?" "You must take responsibility for your appearance," but, "You're *not* going out looking like that!" "You need to play sports and be involved with extracurricular activities and be popular with all the kids," but, "You're *never* home!" When we do this, our children feel torn about meeting (and yet always seem to fall short of) our expectations. They can't ever seem to win. Increasingly, we are seeing young people with ulcers, psychological problems and stress-related illnesses. We must remember that they desperately want to please us, even at the cost of their own physical and mental health. We need to stop and look at what our rules are doing to them. Why are we demanding so much so soon?

RULE 4: Let them make their own rules sometimes; or, even better, why not form rules together as a family so that some aspect of life together is simpler? After all, rules can make things smoother, less conflict-ridden. My favorite in our home is this one: Whoever cooks dinner gets out of doing dishes. Here's another: Whoever did the mess gets to clean it up. For the jobs no one likes, we take turns.

How can we improve the rule-making in our lives? First, by recognizing how very many we seem to have and by looking to cut some of them back. Then, we need to examine whether or not we judge others by the rules we've made but have neglected to tell them. Often it's violations of these that cause us to judge another person badly. Because someone has forgotten to pick up doesn't mean they're a slob or lazy; they may just have been called away to something more urgent. Or, maybe they're not finished yet ... or maybe they're discouraged and in need of a word of support. Rules get in the way of relationships when they lead to judgments. Instead, we need to address the situation and offer to help. Perhaps taking a moment just to listen can set things right again.

Rules are at their best when they make life easier, safer, or more secure. When they become an end unto themselves, they destroy relationships and create conflict. If people-growing is our business in families, then we must take time to examine whether or not the rules we make support this important effort.

When We Don't Agree

"**O**UR PROBLEM as parents is that we don't agree on how to do it," a young mom said as she confessed her confusion and frustration.

"I tell our daughter to pick up, and he tells her it's OK to keep playing. I get crazy!"

No two people parent the same way. No two, despite their love for one another and their children, see or judge or decide things the same way.

What does this do to the children? It confuses them. They wonder whose word will prevail. So they test the disciplinary waters. First, they try the shallower, easier option to see what will happen next. If they abruptly find themselves in deep waters, they wonder how they got there and avoid doing it again.

This means that, when a problem arises for them, they look at the authorities around them to decide which course to take, not at the problem and its components. The child's agenda is shifted away from "How should I solve this dilemma?" to "How is my parent going to react when I do it this way?"

If it's permission they seek, the question raised in the child's mind is "Which parent will say what I want them to say?" rather than "Which course of action is the wisest to pursue?"

The energy involved in a child's trying to second-guess parents is considerable. To do it well, the youngster must be able to read body language, expressions, tones of voice, body tension, time of day, circumstance and mood. Needless to say, they are masters at this. They come in on the mark nearly every time. When they fail, it's probably because their problem is so pressing that their assessment of our condition is clouded by stress.

How do we get children to focus on solving their problems rather than play one parent against the other to achieve victory? We talk with one another. We check in with our spouse the moment a "suspicious" request is made. We say, "Let me check with your mom/dad before I get back to you with our answer."

Never argue with one another about a disciplinary strategy when the children are present. Go to a quiet, private place together; exit only after you have agreed on a compromise position that will establish a good precedent and the kind of value-building experience you want for your child.

"United we stand" … but only when we're in a dilemma which presents a set of constructive options any of which might be chosen to resolve the problem.

If, however, one parent is proposing a solution which can damage the child, the other parent *must* step in to protect the child. When mom or dad is beating, embarrassing, humiliating or discouraging the child, the other adult is the youngster's only available ally. Children are rarely able to defend themselves under these circumstances and easily incur damage; the threat of damage to children or young people cannot be tolerated by responsible adults.

If we need to stop the other parent, we should just do that, *stop* them. We should not humiliate one another in front of the children, call names, hit or put down. We must just say, "Stop doing that. We need to talk." And then go do it. Talk until the issue is settled. The child who has watched one parent hurt him terribly while the other just stands by is frequently more injured by the "do-nothing" parent than by the abusive one. Violence has no place in good parenting.

Children need parents united in promoting their best welfare. This leaves room for a great variety of parenting styles, but it never allows parents to hurt the child. When an issue is in doubt, parents can talk, negotiate, compromise and cooperate. It's a huge job; it seems unending. It requires two people working together, not two tugging apart.

Forgiveness

WE STRUGGLE to do our growing-up work. We're "on" 24 hours a day. When we fail or things don't go 100 percent as planned we shoulder the additional burden of being wrong, of having screwed up.

"You can only do the best you can do!" It's a chorus we recite to one another at work. It's at least some small comfort.

But there's a better way. We can forgive. First ourselves, then others.

How do we do this? How do we teach our children to do this? To teach it we must do it. We must practice with them the process of forgiveness. It's a healing thing.

THE CHILD CAME to spend his special time with Mom that night as usual. They would read together, taking turns, laughing and trying on different voices. It was their bedtime ritual. They'd talk and share and look back over things which happened that day. It was a time they each treasured.

But this night would be different. Instead of reading the book he had brought, he said he wanted to talk.

First Mom and son spoke of the kids in the neighborhood, about sportsmanlike behavior, about frustrations when certain young-sters refused to accept rules of play, about the trials these young ones were suffering at home, about hostilities toward one another.

Suddenly, the son turned away, curled up in a ball, and began sobbing. Something had just gone terribly wrong! Mom had not a clue about the child's abrupt transformation. The evening had been going so well. But something had triggered a cataclysm of feelings wholly unexpected and startling.

"Honey, tell me! What's happening inside you? Something's wrong." She moved quickly, urgently, with pleading words and gestures. Her response seemed as dramatic as his own.

His body reacted in severe discomfort. He twisted as if in pain, edged imperceptibly away from her, and tightened the body ball he'd made.

"No, Mom, you'll be mad! I did something a long time ago, and I never told you. It was so horrible you could never forgive me. Please don't make me tell. I was bad, and I try never to think about it; but, sometimes it pops up, and I feel awful all over again." His words came in spurts, agonized and shame-filled.

Mom knew about unforgiveness. She'd spent many times in her own life reaching deep into her spirit, seeking out those guilt-ridden memories that held her down in subtle and leaden ways.

"Please dig inside, honey. Tell me your story. I promise I will forgive you." She knew it was a pact she could keep. She could forgive him anything.

Her arms reached around him, holding him extra tight, as he slowly, by fits and starts, untangled his recurring waking nightmare. As he did, she soothed, stroked his hair, urged him onward. She felt his pain almost as if she herself bore it.

After he'd finished unraveling his tale, the two hugged. A strange, relieved, quiet peacefulness descended on them.

When the silence leveled out, Mom began tenuously. She spoke to her son about the cause-effect connections he had made, perhaps erroneously, at the early age during which the incident had occurred.

Together, they examined the evidence, wondered if he had jumped to the wrong conclusions about his culpability in the matter, and finally decided there was no way to find out for sure.

"You must know that having made a mistake way back there doesn't mean you're not a good and gentle person," Mom waited for his listening. He'd heard. Good.

"How has your attitude, the one you didn't like from way back then, changed?" Mom sought to draw something learned and grown and changed from his backward glance.

"Oh, I never, ever, ever think like that or would do that ever, ever again," he was adamant.

"Do you need for me to forgive you?" Mom had to make sure the unfinished business was laid to rest.

He nodded gently. "Yeah, Mom."

"Then, I forgive you, Honey. If you did what you think, I forgive you." They hugged.

"And if you didn't, I forgive you for thinking badly of yourself."

Silence. Wonderfully clear, light silence. Then a grin.

"G'night, Mom! And thanks. I haven't felt this good for a long time. I like when we have our special-time talks."

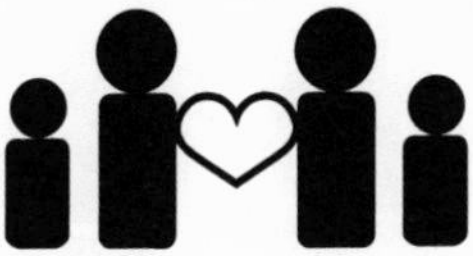

About Dishwashing

ONE OF OUR children recently visited the home of a friend. After a snack, the friend and our son put their used dishes into the host's dishwasher. It came to our son's mind that we had one but hadn't used it in years. The friend was surprised. He wondered why we'd never had it repaired.

"Doing dishes keeps our family together," our son replied after a moment's thought on the matter.

Needing help to get everything done is not a contrivance in our home. We must have their help to keep pace with our weekly chores. My husband and I both work full time, and we have four children. We're not alone. Most families attempting to pay for food, lodging and clothes are finding that everyone has to pitch in.

Every fall we get a grapple load of uncut logs that needs to be sliced up with our chainsaw, split and stacked so that we can save on heating costs during the cold New England winter. It's always been a full family effort, with our children planning weekends home from college to get the job done. Even visitors don work gloves, generate a healthy outdoor sweat and eat the hearty meals I serve. The hard work enlarges appetites that require prompt satisfaction. It's amazing how much gets consumed with hard work and fresh air.

Neighbors fascinated by this phenomenon have been known to line up by the roadside, watching and making various inconsiderate comments to the laborers. Someday we're going to charge big bucks for the privilege!

It's fun. My husband has the wonderful capacity to turn work into laughter. When his sparkle and good humor enter the "chores scene," those he's snagged get lured into the feeling that they're at play. Energy levels rise, and the work gets done like wildfire.

One family I know turns dishwashing time into a sportspage-reading event. While the rest of the members scrape, wash, dry and put away, one goes through scores, play-offs and championship standings.

Cleaning out closets in another home deteriorates into full-scale clothing swaps.

Helping to sort toys and putting some into attic storage can produce hours of fantasy play and happy recall. Where did this come from? Remember when Gram took us to the toy store for this? Oh, there's that piece I thought was lost ... and on it goes.

A young mom I just met tells me that she never asks her 5-year-old daughter to pick up her room. Amazed, I wondered if she did it for her or, perhaps, had a magic formula I'd better find out.

"I tell her that, should she need me in the middle of the night, I couldn't make it from her bedroom door to her bed. If she could just clear a small path for me, I could reach her without breaking my neck," she explained. Smart mom.

She continued, "But she never stops with just clearing the path. In no time at all she gets fascinated, starts putting a book back on a shelf, sorting through her puzzle pieces, getting the playhouse people back in their respective playrooms and has most of the room in good order." Sneaky, huh?

Cooking meals together frequently produces unexpected improvised dishes with taste thrills, some unreproducible–gratefully.

Decorating for holidays when done all together may not result in House Beautiful, but it will surely create an environment in which everyone feels welcome.

Our littlest recently suggested to his grandmother that she might really enjoy helping him dust; she could hold the cloth while he sprayed it, and then she could wipe the tables. Being the wise woman she is, Grammy decided to go shopping with me, instead.

Doing yard work gives each family member the opportunity to bite off whichever chunk of property maintenance he or she wants. There's enough for all. No one need feel left out.

Even when we're down to just the regular old routine chores, we are always able to give choices: Would people like to shop, do laundry, vacuum, dust, make beds or pick up the living areas? We can't guarantee 100 percent funtime, but we usually can generate just enough energy to get the process rolling; it's sheer physical inertia that's hardest to overcome.

"The family that does dishes together stays together," I read beneath our son's recounting of his dishwasher conversation. It's about more than just having clean kitchenware; it's also about having time to reconnect, to talk things out, to build family memories and to enjoy being together.

Family is about cooperating and community building.

Saying Thank-You

I HATE STANDING over a reluctant youngster struggling to write thank-you notes. That's what I'm doing right now, and it's not a pleasant task. It is an important one, though. I wish I had some wonderful formula to make it go easier, but I can't come up with one that's designed to work every time.

Sometimes guilt works. I start with the "think what they had to go through to get this present for you" routine until their eyes roll up into their heads. Then I stop.

"Hounding" seldom works very well. But if you *do* use it, dish it out sparingly and unexpectedly. Don't be surprised if at these times, you suddenly see them rush forth, take up the pen and start writing "Dear ..." on clean, white paper. You'll wonder if you're in the right house.

Sitting with them ahead of time to rehearse what they'll write eases the painful process of composing. Remember the formula letters we used to write? Wouldn't it be nice if we could encourage our children to be a bit more spontaneous in their thank-yous?

We have many artists in our family, so their letters are often pictures with sparse writing on them. "Thank you" is, after all, the heart of the message; as long as that's clearly present, the gratitude has been adequately communicated.

When all else fails, we call. I know it's letting them off the hook, but often this mode of thanksgiving suits everyone's pleasure. Frequently it's long distance, and so it's our adult thank-you as well.

But why all this fuss and bother? Why should we care so much that our children express their thanks?

Many years ago, a young mother-to-be friend was observing

my interaction with our little children. After a short while she inquired, puzzled, "Why do you always insist they say 'Please' and 'Thank you'?"

Somehow this, didn't fit with what she saw as my rather non-traditional parenting style, and she was curious why I'd not thrown these pleasantries out, too. I stopped to reconsider what I'd been doing and decided there was good reason to keep this practice alive in our children: a grateful heart appreciates its blessings and remains humble and human. Valuing one's small efforts on our behalf is a skill important to develop in family relationships.

My husband tells me it's good business practice, too. In a management workshop he recently attended, he spoke of being especially impressed by a presenter who urged participants to take the time and care to thank others for their kindnesses on the job. He told them they should write short notes of gratitude regularly; this could result in a more gracious and gentle work place.

We often reflect that it's the little things that make or break our day-to-day existence. Instead of being quick to criticize or put down or complain, perhaps we should take a moment to look through those things others do for us which we haven't noticed for a while.

"Thanks for taking care of your dishes." "I really appreciated that you called to say you were coming home late." "You were good to remember that your milk money was due today. I forgot all about it." "I'm grateful you went to bed all by yourself tonight."

It's the little things that matter and, it's the thank-yous that give us the energy to keep doing them.

Giving Children Back
Their Own Problems

A PROFESSIONAL CALLED about one family's strug-gle with their teen. "Mom and Dad are so very good. Their son is being outrageous. He's going out with a young woman who is just plain bad for him."

"The situation has escalated to the young man's threatening to move out and live with his sweetheart. Neither has any money or a place to stay, and they're both still in school," she went on. "How can such these parents have such difficulties? They've always done everything for him."

Maybe that's at the core of the problem. "Doing for" just doesn't produce responsible, thinking, independent youngsters.

And then another:

A young mom, distraught at not having accomplished toilet training with her 3-year-old, was getting worried it would never happen. She had visions of the daughter going to school in dia-pers or wetting in public and embarrassing everyone.

"Whenever I sit to chat with other young mothers in morning coffee clatches, I hear them boast of their 2-year-olds being trained; I feel like a failure."

I remembered how intimidating this was in my own young-mother years. But, my cowardly solution was to stop attending such gatherings. It seemed that no one there subscribed to my doctor's advice; I felt unsupported, lonely and inept.

A certain amount of healthy self-doubt, however, is good for the soul. It challenges us to revisit our position and attack our stand from other points of view. Often the result is a more bal-anced, convinced or flexible posture and a resolve to accomplish the desired end.

This young mom decided to make sure toilet training happened through every effort she possessed. She read books on the topic, decided to implement to the letter the advice proposed in one of them, and, when that failed, determined to remind her daughter regularly through her day that she needed to sit on the toilet.

"If I don't tell her, she will not go on her own!" she agonized. "Is something wrong with her? Will she never be trained?"

Watching the youngster playing happily with others, I saw she was precocious and alert to her personal environment. Perhaps a check with the pediatrician would be wise as a first step, but I questioned whether that were the real problem.

Mom had taken responsibility for the training, but the daughter had not.

"Ask her to tell you when she feels grown up enough to take on going to the bathroom all by herself with no reminders from you," I suggested.

"But she'll have accidents," mom protested.

"Isn't it O K to make mistakes while you're learning?" I questioned.

Mom immediately caught on. Of course, it was O K with her! Once this concept was offered, mom knew what her strategy would be.

She would explain to her daughter that the job for big people was to take care of their own toileting, that sometimes mistakes would happen, but that mom would not nag/remind/cajole her any longer. It was appropriately *her* job, and only *she* could do it.

Mom's role had just shifted to "helpmate," "cheerleader," supporter; mom knew that this meant she had to trust the youngster enough to leave it with her to accomplish the growth at hand.

As we worked through this young mother's dilemma, I wished I could have chatted with the older mom and dad whose son was causing them so much pain. With my limited information, I felt they, too, would have to play the same role ... a bit late, but necessary nevertheless.

"I don't feel good about your choices right now. I think they're unwise and will hurt you. But I recognize that you must try them out. And you must bear the consequences of what you do." That would be a first step to consider.

Then, the second step must follow: "Know that, regardless of what happens, we love you. We will always be here, not to bail you out, but to stand with you and be of support in encouraging you to follow through on your responsibility."

Children & Religion

"WE DON'T go to church. We want our children to pick their own religion when they grow up; we don't want to impose our faith onto them." How often I hear this! And those who say it truly believe, what they're saying.

But let's look at how children learn their life habits. They grow up experiencing life as they live it. They watch, mimic, listen, enjoy, participate and draw meaning from those most vital to their lives. Parents and family members form the core of those they model.

If we think for a moment how we rear our children, we discover that we rely heavily on our own memories of having been parented. The patterns established with our parents lie deep within our most intuitive responses to what our children do. If we can make these subconscious patterns conscious we find we can choose to accept or reject repeating what they did. We can start changing what we do with our youngsters. It's hard to create brand new patterns, to try the untried, to risk the unknown.

Churchgoing is one of these family "habits" difficult to create out of nothing. It involves a blending, an integration of the faith dimension into every fabric of life. It implies "telling the story" of an entire people, a tradition, an expectation, a view of life and its value when lived out, both in our homes and our communities.

If we want our children to even consider church as the living out of their spiritual dimension, we must introduce it by living it with them. We must go to church with them regularly, share our faith traditions with them, encourage their "looking within" for the source of truth and peace and love, and speak willingly and openly of our own personal response to faith. We must dare to live out the values of caring for others and for creation. Children watch as we live and participate in our faith.

Yes, it's personal. But it's also social. Church is community. It's both horizontal and vertical. This truth must be communicated by each of us in our own tongue. For some, the medium might be singing and playing sacred music; for others, standing or kneeling or dancing in worship; sometimes it's being silent in the face of a magnificent sky or a beautiful flower. It absorbs our whole existence and leaves us clean, restored, reconciled and refreshed. It's living out our credo by treating each another with dignity. It's a way of living that transcends the superficial and seeks to find deeper meaning.

If we hesitate introducing it to our children, we might deprive them of a critical life tool. Those individuals whose spirituality has been nurtured over their lifetimes frequently are better able to face tragedy, turmoil and loss. They look beyond the concrete realities they experience and find meaning otherwise lost to them.

Every culture we've known has sought the meaning of life. Children never introduced to their own spirituality are poor indeed. It's the "stuff" of dreams, hopes, joys, peace, true commitment and transcendence. It stands in sharp contrast to our shrewd, commercial, self-centered marketplace. But it holds out to our tired spirits the courage and energy we need to make a difference.

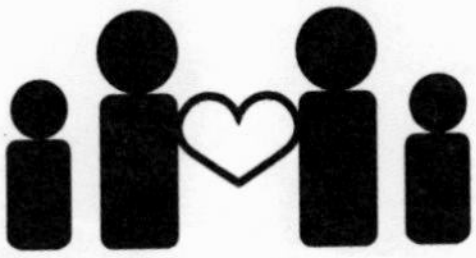

Helping Children Understand Death

HOLIDAYS FREQUENTLY bring with them memories of those separated by distance, circumstance or death. Children, especially the very young, are understandably puzzled by the absence of these loved ones. It's at times like these that we get questions that are hard to answer. Ones involving death are the most difficult.

We want to avoid exposing children to the details, hoping to spare them undue anxiety; on the other hand, we want to reassure them, should this be our belief, that the departed have gone to a better place and are at peace.

Since the young seek out our answers to this most puzzling of life's mysteries, we need to explore how they understand what we might tell them.

First, children know only as much as they've experienced. Their worlds are concrete and real. They continually construct cause-effect connections that explain what they see and hear; they attempt to predict what will happen next so they can establish security and confidence.

They also rely deeply on family and close friends to support, reassure and warn of danger. The very thought of separation from loved ones causes anxiety and insecurity.

Their concept of God is unclear and subject to magical, often disconnected thinking. They suspect it has something to do with the heavens and celestial bodies and powerful forces. They listen hard to what we say and desperately seek to comprehend how all our explanations fit into their cloudy scheme of the physical world.

Finally, we must understand that when they hear our words,

they also "hear" our feelings and attitudes. If we find ourselves unsure of certain details we give them, we must say so. If we give them information about which we are confident, however, we must be ready to reassure. Reality, though vital to their development, is often scary. Consequently, it must be doled out using words and concepts clear to children their age and should make sense based on what they already know. If we watch their faces intently, we'll get from them the clues we need to guide our explanations.

"Grammy has gone to heaven," we say. But to a young child, "heaven" connects with the sky and flying. When Dad prepares to go catch his plane for a business trip, the youngster reacts with panic. After all, Grammy went to heaven and didn't return; he won't, either!

"God came to get him in the night. Why? Because God wanted him to be in heaven with Him," often translates as confusion to the child. What sort of God is this who takes those we love away from us whenever He wants their company?

"He sleeps (in the Lord)" frequently translates into terror for young children. If sleeping can result in death, they want no part of it! Youngsters who don't normally balk at bedtime routines suddenly begin a fierce clinging and hysterical crying. Little do the attending adults realize that their own unconscious euphemism has once again communicated the wrong message. Rather than feeling reassured that death is peaceful for some, the child fears it could happen to him at any time and for no reason other than pure fatigue.

Whenever we attempt to explain a loved one's death to children, we must take care to give them information that is real and related to the body's function. For example, children understand that the heart pumps blood throughout the body. If that muscle stops, the blood won't flow anymore, food won't get to all the other body parts, and they'll stop working, too. Death means that everything the body does has stopped.

The information we give children must match their ability to understand based on the limited experience they've had with the physical world. The words we use should not be metaphorical or theological or allegorical. As much as possible, they should reflect our knowledge of the child's vocabulary. They should be crystal clear, should contain no double meanings, and should be accurate.

Death: A Family Affair

DEATH IS a family affair. When it comes to us, we must respond with openness, inclusiveness and grace. Just as the loved one was part of the life shared in the family, so also should the deceased be embraced by those surviving in the family. Each member mourns according to his or her own capacity, perception and style; this is as it should be and is best honored and respected by the support community.

Every member should be given the opportunity to know as soon as possible when death has happened. Children should not be sheltered. They deserve to be trusted with the basic facts related to the death; they should be treated with openness and care so that they can begin to comprehend that life is precious and delicate.

Last week my husband's mom died. She suffered a heart attack four days earlier, was hospitalized, and had the opportunity to visit several times with each of us before the second attack occurred. Even our 6-year-old was able to be with her for a brief time. She showed him the oxygen tubes and IVs, explained how they were helping her to breathe better and give her the medications she required.

When the telephone rang at 1:30 A.M., our eldest son took the call. He had been unable to sleep, sensing something was amiss. Each of us in our own way knew that Grammy's time was at hand. Our daughter, returning from a Washington, D.C. crew meet, sensed she should pray for grandmother at around midnight. We were all connected, somehow, even before we knew the truth.

As morning dawned, our little Ben awoke and went straight to his dad, who broke the news to him. Our son had been especially close to Grammy, so his tears came instantaneously. He then sought me out. We hugged, cried, and rocked together.

The questions began right away. How did she die? What is a heart attack? Why does a person die if it is too severe? What happens to the person's body at death? Does it stay warm? Can Grammy still see? Does she still breathe? Can she feel anything? What should we do next?

With each question, my husband and I tried our best to respond accurately and with sensitivity to his level of understanding. You could see his little face mirror concern, confusion and comprehension. Sometimes tears would trickle down his cheeks and then fade before the next wave came upon him.

As we prepared for the visiting hours, we offered Ben the chance to see his grandmother laid out in the coffin. He wanted to go. Cautiously, we took him with us for the private family viewing. As he approached the casket, he at first seemed unsure but then decided to come close. He touched her hand, felt her cheek, knelt down, and desperately tried to absorb the reality before him.

We made it clear that he could leave at any time, and that one of our older children would be glad to stay with him back at our home until we returned. He chose to stay with us. From time to time, he would come to one of us for a hug. We frequently repeated our offer to let him return home; but he refused. He cordially greeted friends and listened to warm stories about the woman he loved so dearly. He seemed to gain comfort and a sense that he was playing an important part in the life of his family.

During the funeral Mass, Ben helped his cousin bring up the bread and wine; our eldest son read the scripture passages; my husband and his brother draped the coffin with the white pall; our daughter helped choose parts of the liturgy; our second son, a saxophonist, and I, at the organ, provided the liturgical music. We were each able by using our gifts to express feelings and to participate fully in the solemn event before us.

Following the internment we invited those who had attended to partake with us in the mercy meal. Everyone pitched in. They carefully arranged trays filled with meats, fruits and cheeses; they poured coffee, washed dishes, re-loaded bowls of chips, and reminisced about the good times. Perfect strangers became co-workers, and laughter filled our ample kitchen.

Our family seemed to grow closer in the midst of the flurry. With each new joy and sorrow it seems we have another chance to respond with care and support and understanding. Resting securely beneath the changes, though, is a commitment to openness and the recognition of each new reality. Rooted in our sense that family is at the core of belonging and working together, we can face the most difficult of times and be sustained.

The Guinea Pig

BEN'S GUINEA PIG died. It happened one Saturday morning. We were sleeping, and a distraught Benjamin, age 5, appeared at our bedside with an almost-limp little animal. He laid him on our blanket and urged him to walk. The guinea pig seemed to be losing energy before our very eyes. Within a short time, he stopped moving.

Ben wept as if his heart was breaking. It was. "But I loved him", he sobbed. "He was my own very first pet. He was so nice...." The litany continued as he tried to comprehend the reality before him. The warm little body turned slowly stiff and cold. I cried with him, and we hugged tight and long. Words somehow held no power to comfort, and I felt the awful emptiness Ben was feeling inside.

I felt pride, too. Ben was showing me through his mourning, which continued intermittently throughout the next few days, that he had been deeply attached to this small animal and that he truly missed it. Missing can only happen when love has happened first.

As weeks went by, the sharpness of the loss seemed to lessen and a dull ache took its place. Ben spoke more of what the little animal had meant to him; he recalled the details of his noisy squeaks, the softness of his fur, the mass of black and orange and white cowlicks covering his body, the white tuft of hair that stuck out of his forehead giving him the appearance of a certified unicorn. He laughed about these things and about the good times he'd had sharing the guinea pig with teachers and friends. Now his pet was gone forever.

In the midst of all this, I thought I detected a quality of new sweetness in his musings. His outlook had changed subtly, and I was not terribly surprised when I heard his tenuous, "Mom, could we think about getting another pet for me?"

He'd done his work well. Ben had allowed himself to feel deeply the event he'd witnessed, to "go with the flow" of his mourning process, to face the hurt that love always seems to bring in its wake, and to risk loving again. He was ready to go on.

Through all of Ben's experiences I, too, wept, remembered, laughed and considered new beginnings. But something of the events we'd witnessed together on that Saturday morning stayed with me: How fragile is this thing we call life, how precious, how out of our ability to control. There are things we can't fix, problems we can't solve, aches that must be endured and memories that cannot be erased. There's always some new reality, though, disguised beneath these, waiting to be discovered.

So, what is our proper response as parents to such things? Inevitabilities are a part of our children's lives. Do we, in our desire to comfort, say, "It'll be all right. Don't cry; tomorrow you'll feel better…." Or, wanting to fix it, do we suggest that we buy the child a new one right away so that she/he will forget the beloved one just gone? Are we really listening, or are we so uncomfortable with our powerlessness that we attempt to "take charge" and get everybody back "in control?"

Our most realistic and loving response is to stand with our children at these times, to allow ourselves to feel with them, to risk with them, to listen for the messages they try so hard to communicate, to respect them enough to know that they'll come to their own solutions, and to be ready when they're ready to move on.

Why do I get the feeling that something in me was healed, too; that Ben wasn't the only one who learned one more piece of this mystery we call living?

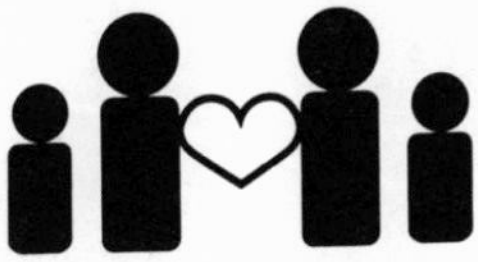

Translating the World
to Our Children

CHILDREN don't magically know what to do. They need instruction. When social events or circumstances arise, they don't always know what we expect of them or what purpose the events serve. We want to give our children the chance to be who they are, but we also expect them to know intuitively what is happening around them and how to do the "right thing."

Part of our role as parents is to translate for them what is going on and what people should do in response. Children really need some information from time to time that will help them to act appropriately; sometimes they need access to the reality of people's actions, their expressions, their words. This is part of their social education and something we can transmit to them as no one else can.

To do this, we must be aware that their life experience is limited, that they see things happening that bring no particular meaning to their existing mental structures, that they're puzzled.

So, before we expose them to a new event, we might want to preview it for them. We can tell them what we know will be happening, in what order, why it will occur that way, what it means, and how they might respond. This arms them with a framework of information around which the unexpected can be dealt with more easily.

Let's take a look at an example. We are planning a visit to a large museum in Boston. Lots of people will be viewing many exhibits on several floors. We might tell them what sorts of art pieces they'll see, whether or not they may touch them, how to walk and not run or jump, where they can go if they lose us, how long we'll be there, and what amount of money we'll spend on items from the gift shop. If we do this ahead of time and give them a chance to ask questions, our trip will go more smoothly and there'll be less need to correct behavior in public.

Translating the world to our children never seems to stop; it just seems to get a bit more involved and complicated as they grow older. It's fun to watch them use us more and more as life encyclopedias once they reach adulthood. One friend confessed that his parents seemed to get smarter and smarter as he approached his mid-twenties!

Their questions tumble forth and astound us:

"How do I go about getting a good piano teacher? How'd you ever find mine?"

"I'd like to vote this year; where do I register? Can I vote right away?"

"How do I look for a good, affordable car? Can I get a loan? How much will I have to put down? Will you co-sign for me? What kind of insurance will I need? Can I hook into your policy?"

In attacking questions such as these, parents sometimes need the wisdom of Solomon. They can lay out the information they have accumulated about the topic, mention the various options open under the circumstances, narrow down to several good ones and why these are preferable, and then ask the young person what she thinks would be a sensible course of action.

Telling them outright what they ought to do doesn't work as well; they become dependent on us for their decisions and can blame us if things don't work to their satisfaction. "Processing" with them is the best teaching for this worthy end.

If our children are not coming to us for help, we might gently ask them whether or not they have a plan for the action they're about to undertake. If they do, and if they choose to share it with us, we must be careful not to shoot it down or discourage them. They have every legitimate right to make their own mistakes. We need to grant them that privilege. And it's never OK to say "I-told-you-so!" If we do, they'll never consult us again.

Just one more dictum, and I'll be done ... *don't lecture!* In case there's any doubt, children give us a huge clue when we're doing it: their eyes roll vaguely up into their heads and glaze with disinterest. Antidote: Cease speaking immediately, mid-sentence, and exit stage left!

We can't live our children's lives for them, but we can be of great assistance in helping them become competent adults. Translating the world to our children is part of our teaching role as parents. It also cements our relationship with them as they move into adulthood.

Parenting for Peace

PEACE BEGINS at home. Are we teaching and living it with our children? If not, how can we expect that our children will seek it in the world ahead? As we grow older, theirs will be the power to make it happen.

Television news seems aglow with reporting skirmishes, guerrilla attacks, bombing aftermaths, grisly scenes of mangled bodies, and sidewalks stained in human blood. There is no better time than now to take a penetrating look into how we live as family: Are we promoting a real and urgent understanding of the peace process in our homes? Below is the beginning of a checklist to get us started in a self-examination.

- When a child hurts another, do we first soothe, comfort, and console the injured, or do we give our first attention to the aggressor, thereby reinforcing that behavior?
- Do we "feel with" our children when they are hurt, or do we reject them and their injuries by using phrases like, "It's nothing, don't cry. It doesn't hurt."
- Do we accept one another's feelings, or do we say, "Don't feel that way. It's not nice." Feelings are neither bad nor good; they just are. It's when we act on them to hurt others that we can be judged.
- Do we let our children and spouses own their problems? Do we respect them enough to trust that only they can solve their dilemmas? Do we restrict ourselves to listening empathetically?
- Do we dare to apologize, to ask forgiveness, to admit that we've made a mistake, or must we always be right? Reconciliation is a bountiful gift in family.
- Do we consider another's privacy, point of view and priorities,

just as we expect that ours will be considered?

- When problems arise, do we attempt to compromise, negotiate and reach consensus instead of always having to win? Can we bend?
- Are we tolerant when others are preoccupied with their own thoughts and we want them to join us in our feelings? Do others always have to be "with us," or can we let them just be where they are?
- Do we try to keep the realities of war away from our children, or do we acknowledge that our detached technology kills and maims, that it's not just a movie with special effects? People die, and their loved ones cry out in horror. That's real.
- Do we speak of our deep sadness over this war, or do we think it's not a topic for children?
- Do we treasure life in our homes and neighborhoods and towns, or do we live our lives unconnected to the lives of others?
- Are we respectful of our environment by learning how to treasure and maintain it, or do we expect that someone else will do it, that it's not our business?
- Do we actively pursue learning about those who are different from us, or do we just dismiss them as strange or peculiar because of religion, color, physical condition, mode of dress, economic or social condition?
- Are we working toward a global awareness of our interconnectedness by reading newspapers, watching geographic programs, visiting museums, supporting efforts at greater international understanding? Do we have and use globes, atlases and maps of regions in the news?
- Do we let our children join in our discussions of world events?
- Do we carefully consider what they think? Do we value their points of view, or are we condescending in our attitudes toward their thinking, dismissing it as insignificant?
- Do we speak up for those whose rights are being violated, or, by our silence, do we inflict our prejudices on our children?

- Do we reach out materially to those who are experiencing trouble, or do we blame them for their misfortune?
- Do we treat one another fairly, or do we play favorites, extending our graciousness only to those we prefer? Do we apply the limits we set in our homes equally to all ages, sexes, temperaments and personalities, or are we softer on one person than we are on another?

Peace joins hands with justice in our parenting. It seeks openness, hopefulness, reconciliation and inclusiveness. It embraces and accepts, knowing that to survive it must begin at home.

Homework Hassles

PARENTS SHOULDN'T do their children's homework for them. Sounds reasonable, doesn't it? Someone, somewhere in our collective past, however, has told us that we should. Aren't we as parents responsible for our children's success in school? Isn't our job during their school years to stand glaring over them, insisting that they do their work perfectly as soon as they get home; otherwise they mustn't play outside ever again, right?

Can we try another scenario? How about this: They come home exhausted from a hard day at school, and we greet them with cookies and milk. They unwind: watching a half-hour of TV; making a brief call to a friend about what happened today; listening to easy music; going for a quick ride on the bike.

Sometimes the child's greatest need upon arriving home is to have a ready ear waiting to listen. We don't need to provide solutions. Simply appreciating the child's experiences can provide the de-briefing so desperately needed.

Home should be a haven, a place where we are received warmly and with understanding. This is not to be mistaken for a my-child-right-or-wrong attitude, but rather a place a child can take comfort just being him/herself. Besides, if children have to use their energy fighting parents and schoolmates, they'll have none left with which to absorb their lessons.

If parents shouldn't hover and nag, should they just leave their children alone? No. A lack of interest communicates a lack of caring. Because being ignored is so awful, the child sometimes resorts to outrageous behavior for attention; or worse, the child reads from parental non-interest that the youngster is unimportant and worthless. If the child begins to believe this, he/she will sink into depression and discouragement; soon the child stops trying and fades into the social background.

What, then, is a parent's best strategy for dealing with homework? First, adults should give children a break at their homecoming. Then, parents should show interest in what work has been assigned and can cross-check to make sure the assignment has been properly understood.

Clearing the environment to make it conducive to mental activity, children get the message that what they're doing is important and that we won't interrupt their efforts. Chores can wait until the schoolwork is completed. This concession tells them that lessons take priority but that home will also need their attention before they're done.

Should we listen to spelling words and times tables? Of course. We can check their work on request, too; but we should never correct it for them. At the most, we can point out where their errors lie; but they should be responsible for correcting them. We can help them plan ahead for long-range assignments by giving them calendars and helping them determine what needs to be done and how far ahead.

What if they can't figure out their work? Should we attempt to teach them our methods? Step cautiously here, please. Generally, we should encourage them to ask their teachers to explain it again the next morning. The purpose of homework is to determine whether or not the child has understood the work presented in class.

Do we draw their maps and illustrations for them? No. We can cheer-lead and encourage and chauffeur to the local library and give hints (if they ask) about how the work might be done better, but we never do it for them.

Should we type their reports if they ask? My mother's heart bleeds here. I do typing sometimes. But I have conditions: I need advanced warning, and it must not be a typing class assignment.

So, here's the bottom line: Give them time to unwind; listen;

show sincere interest; encourage; let them take responsibility for accomplishing their own work. That's the only way they'll have any pride in it. Support their efforts, go to meetings and special events, but let the school be the teacher.

Parent Report Card

ONE NIGHT last week Benjamin came home with two bright yellow papers headed, "Report Card for Parents." First thing the next morning we saw him huddled over the dining table, guarding his work and intensely circling letters next to statements arranged in a long column.

He carefully rated each category of parent behavior, assigning letter grades and concluding with the proud delivery of his finished product to us, his eagerly awaiting parents.

I should explain further. There were directions for us, too. Running the length of the third column, outside the boxed evaluation section, we were told that this document should be a springboard to parent-child dialogue for greater mutual understanding.

"Now, don't get upset, parent," it spoke authoritatively. "What you perceive is often different from what the child means. Talk it out."

So far, so good, I thought. After all, why not give the child power to declare his or her appreciation of the parents' role? This theory was great, but it soon raised the hair on the back of my neck as it played out.

As I scanned the document so proudly delivered, I saw my "D" before I saw any other grade. It was accusing me of not caring about his appearance.

"What?!" My reaction was confused, hurt, angry, outraged, flustered, defensive. The flood surprised me.

"Now, take it easy," my calm self whispered. "He comes home with report cards all the time. He seems to take them quite reasonably. My response is always measured, encouraging, highlighting the best grades, the improved areas, the teacher's complimentary comments. He's my son; he'll understand my blubbering."

So, in my most gentle voice, I exploded, "What's this 'D' doing here? I get you nice clothes, keep them clean and in good repair, make sure you shower and scrub the green off your teeth regularly, and examine your lovely face for smears before you go off to school. What's the problem, here?"

Poor kid! His innocent little face stared up at me, stunned.

"You never come to my room and lay out my clothes or help me pick out what to wear in the morning!" he explained hesitantly, I'm sure waiting for the next onslaught.

"You *want* me to do this?" I felt my teeth starting to come out of my mouth.

Just then, I saw my husband slowly descending the stairs toward us. The look on his face cued me in on his own bewilderment. What ghost had he just seen? Complexion pale, control in place, hurt showing ever-so-slightly about the edges, he was holding the insidious yellow paper in his shaking hands.

"Uh, Ben, what's this 'D' under not caring about your appearance?" he managed to mumble between barely moving lips.

Patiently, Ben explained to him what he'd just finished telling me. He was getting experience in standing firm before considerable authority ... in spades!

And he succeeded, too. Right before my eyes I saw Dick's shoulders relax and a smile start to play about the creases in his face.

Later that evening, our daughter came home for a weekend visit from college. Her delight in discovering the report cards was not quiet or sensitive or diplomatic. She roared in laughter at ours and Ben's dilemma.

After Ben had gone to bed, I filled her in. Dick and I planned to report for duty as he chose his clothing for the day.

Ben was thrilled, and Nika (our daughter, a scientist) sat appreciating the scene as she calculated statistical distributions of grades, trends, areas of disparity between the two reports, etc.

You haven't heard about my "A" in preparing tasty meals, my "B" in keeping the house tidy, or my "A" in listening to him and in watching TV with him. Oh, and then I got a "C" for letting him buy what he wants.

I sit looking back on all this now, and I feel the faintest of resentments. Who made up the rating categories, anyway? Some were questionable for their intrinsic value. Did some children get into trouble for their answers? Did parents in the recipient homes compete for grades, compare, feel favored or hurt or circumstantially slighted? Or angry? How was the child's recounting of this experience used back in the classroom?

The taste in my mouth turned from sweet good humor to a tinge of sour. What's wrong with me, anyhow? I should see this exercise with great good grace; but, instead, I'm wary. The parent report card could reinforce some bad parenting habits: playing "buddy" to the child; feeling OK about giving in to children's wants; implying blame and fault rather than applauding the virtues of pitching in; reinforcing sex-linked roles; creating needless conflict in the choice of alternative lifestyles.

Yes, children perceive very differently from adults; they also understand language very differently. Challenge one another we must. But let's respect the individual cultures of our families, honor them; support their best efforts and applaud their successes. Grades have no place in the process.

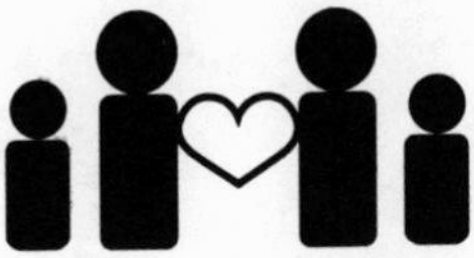

Authority

CHILDREN LEARN about authority from home and parents. As they start going to school they apply and adjust the principles they've acquired to form their own mix. They watch and listen and come home with brand new ideas about authority. These they test on mom and dad.

When we were little, we equated authority with gray hair and status and uniforms. But as we grew up, we discovered that some of the older persons we knew weren't so sure of themselves: some in high office lied and deceived us; some law enforcement professionals broke the law; some elderly cheated and lied.

So we had to decide which authority we would follow, what criteria would determine its validity, and how we would translate it to our children. From our perspective, true authority comes from a kind of integrity and courage; it's doing the right thing by others or self or property. Authority is something we bestow on someone else; it's earned. It's recognized by those with whom we interact.

Did you ever notice that there are some people who seem to command everyone's attention? They embody a kind of respect that makes us want to hear what they have to say. That's earned authority; it's something we give another spontaneously because we recognize a spirit of strength and wisdom – and it's not always age-related.

Genuine authority is balanced. It contains gentleness, understanding, the ability to really hear another speak, and vulnerability alongside the muscle we usually equate with it.

It comes from a person's convictions: personal, ethical, spiritual and social. It is deeply rooted, anchored and sure. It transmits quietly and with confidence. It is used with great care and only in situations requiring limit-setting or correction. It never destroys another; it promotes peaceful resolution and healing. It is just.

We parents must wield it with great prudence and love.

If a child does something wrong, like taking something from another or from a store, we must confront the situation, have the child return the item, pay for it or make restitution in some way, and then drop the matter.

Never should we call the child names such as thief or no-good. These become self-fulfilling prophecies that drive youngsters to do the same thing again. Instead, we tell them we're disappointed and extend our convinced hope that they will act well in the future. We close our disciplinary action by hugging them and loving them without condition. We wrap them in our forgiveness. And we never bring their transgression to mind again.

Children bestow us with authority. They want to know how we feel about the daily experiences they relate to us. Here's where we must be a bit careful. We need to separate our understanding of what they're going through from our judgments of their experiences. Our voices of authority should seek to establish clarity and comfort rather than right/wrong pronouncements.

We must not tell them what to do, how to feel or what to think. They have their own thoughts; if they wish to share them with us, we may consider ourselves fortunate, indeed. Our comments are best restricted to raising questions or voicing concerns or extending genuine appreciation for their experiences. We must not overuse our authority; it is far too precious.

So when a child, especially a young one, misbehaves by hurting him/herself, others, or property, we must take out our strong, determined, convinced voice of disapproval and use it to correct the child. Or, we can allow the child to take initiatives, make mistakes, try new things without having to check in with us for every little thing. This is when our authority shows as the child's "checkpoint" behavior; the youngster wants to share with and be appreciated by us. Our nod of approval has been sought. Our authority has been acknowledged.

Authority, then, comes from within; it is most valid when it is earned and not imposed; it works most effectively when balanced with responsiveness and sensitivity to the child's situation; it should be used to enforce our most profound convictions about the rightness or wrongness of an action; it is lasting only when matched by our living example.

Discipline or Punish?

CHILDREN DON'T ALWAYS behave well. When they don't, we must decide which tool to apply in the situation. Should we discipline or punish to get our point across? Of the two, which one is more effective? Which saves the child's self-esteem so that he/she will grow to produce better behavior? Which creates less resentment and more responsibility-taking? Discipline.

Can you recall a time when you were punished? Was it when you were caught answering Mary's whispered question in class and had to stay after school and write 300 times, "I shall not talk in class?"

Was it the time you got ticketed, chewed out by the judge and fined for being clocked going 15 miles over the limit – all because you were preoccupied about the bills?

Was it the time you were grounded for a curfew broken over circumstances you couldn't control?

I can still remember my parochial school principal coming into our first-grade classroom with an 18-inch ruler to punish any child who'd acted out during the week!

If we look at these, along with others we find painful to recall, we discover a pattern that makes them clearly punishing. Some might be characterized as rulings handed down from an authority exerting power or force upon the less powerful. Frequently, these punitive actions look arbitrary and dependent solely upon the mood of the executor. They're judgmental and allow for no mitigating circumstances.

Punishment humiliates. It reduces its victim to anger and a burning desire for revenge. The injustice of it stays with us long past our specific memory of what we did to provoke it. If chastised in front our friends or those we admire, our loss of face devastates us.

Now, can we remember a time when we were disciplined? Was there an awful incident involving the shattering of our neighbor's window with that pop fly? And, just when we thought we'd be nailed by the man who lived there, he calmly offered to help us replace the broken pane. We never forgot our surprise, and we felt we'd been given a chance to redeem ourselves.

Remember when we crinkled the fender of Mom's prized convertible, and she helped us save enough money to pay for the body work deductible?

Instead of calling us a cheat and confronting us in class, remember that teacher we've always loved who pulled us aside and asked us why we looked over Jimmy's shoulder during the test? Then, to our unending surprise, she gave us a chance to take another test to reestablish our credibility? We never forgot her kindness.

Looking at these examples of discipline gives us very different messages from the ones we got when we were punished. When we were disciplined by someone, we were not destroyed but saved. Our dignity was preserved, not annihilated. We never got away with the misbehavior but were instead given the opportunity to try again or to fix it. We were listened to; we were dealt with honestly and with concern; we were asked to be more responsible or more careful.

When disciplined, we were taught a lesson appropriate to our action. That learning called forth growth and self-restraint; once learned, we were empowered to do better the next time around … and to understand ourselves a bit better.

Scott Peck in his book, "The Road Less Traveled," clarifies the four manifestations of true discipline: the delay of gratification, the taking on of responsibility, the dedication to truth or reality, and balancing. His understanding of discipline calls forth, as little else does, the teaching/guiding role of the parent.

Stimulating growth is much more difficult than putting someone down or grounding him for a week. Feeling the need to control children rather than stimulating and challenging them leads to disrespect and rebelliousness. Capping their resentment with threats eventually backfires and, inevitably, explodes by the time they've reached adolescence.

So, when we consider our response to their misbehavior, we must weigh our decision against this standard: Do we want to hurt them or help them grow?

When we judge, humiliate, compel using fear or force, refuse to listen, or hurt, we are punishing. Children's overwhelming response to this punishment is resentment, or worse.

When we help children to recognize, take responsibility for, learn from, and attempt to make right what's been screwed up, we're acting in a disciplined fashion. And we also teach them well.

Bullies On The Beach

WE VACATION at a campground in Maine. Our seasonal trailer sits on a common circle around which everyone comes and goes.

This year during our stay the house at the mouth of our campground was rented by several families. Belonging to those families were four or five boys aged 10 through 14. Ben, 10, was looking for playmates, and using all his best-tried strategies, he began making overtures to those young people.

Nothing worked. Worse, they undertook a campaign to frighten and intimidate him as he rode solitary along nearby country roads. Jumping out in front of him, calling him names, chasing him on their own bikes, they finally succeeded in completely terrorizing him.

By Tuesday, he had so lost his composure that he came home pedaling like the wind, skidded to a halt at our door, scrambled inside and dropped piteously onto the couch.

"You're really frightened," I opened.

"They scared me to death, Mom," he panted. "Nothing I try seems to work."

My husband and I talked with him some more. Had he really tried it all? Maybe Dad could intervene by riding Ben's bike around hoping to meet them and talk.

Dad stationed himself outside, rode up and down the drive, explored the side roads, all to no avail. Ben burrowed further into his cocoon. Neither of us really blamed him. We were powerless to change the standoff.

Meantime, Dad noticed a young boy, about Ben's age, who seemed alone and was staying with his folks in the back of the campground some distance from the front house. He suggested Ben might want to head back there and introduce himself. Perhaps the two of them could plan some time together and still save a small piece of his vacation.

Ben was agreeable. When they returned from calling on little Jake, I found out that a date had been made to go play on the beach mid-morning the next day. Great!

The pre-appointed rendezvous time came and went. Jake was nowhere. So Ben and I decided we'd go down together, hoping we'd meet up with him along the beach. Dad stayed behind to finish some trailer repairs. He'd join us later.

As we ambled down the sandy incline leading to the water's edge, we saw the families from *the house*. There was shouting, bickering, discontent and conflict hovering like a cloud.

I sighed quietly to myself. "Too bad," I thought.

We continued down the nearly deserted stretch of beach carrying our essentials for the day. The walk would be lengthy, but the panorama we'd grown to love lay as our prize ahead.

Before long, we heard young voices approaching from behind. The boys were coming closer and closer.

More menacing still, they'd each picked up long strands of kelp, smooth, wet and strong, and attached to hose-like flexible stems. As they swished them around us, the boys talked loudly about how it might feel to be slapped by one of these, maybe on the backs of the legs.

Ben and I walked only a few yards more. Our terror had been mounting with each step. I could take it no longer.

"That's *enough!*" I stopped and glared at them. "Put those down." My voice shook. I hoped it didn't show too much.

"*We're* not doing anything!" they protested.

"I'm *not* a fool," I retorted, hoping I was right. "I know that when someone comes up behind you, crowds you, and starts talking about how something they're flashing around can hurt a person, they mean to frighten you."

They were standing stunned, unbelieving. So, I went on.

"If you want to make friends with someone, you don't first scare them to death! You go up to them and introduce yourselves and ask if they'd like to do something fun with you."

One more thought had to be spoken; I quickly added: "That way you don't have to worry about watching your backs all the time." That seemed enough.

Slowly they dropped their "weapons," turned and walked on ahead of us. They were chattering quietly, almost meditatively.

Jake, who was one of them, glanced back and stopped to wait for us. He spoke tenuously to Ben. "I *did* want to pick you up this afternoon."

"But you *didn't* do it," I reminded him. "Friends keep promises they make to one another. Ben was really disappointed you didn't come. He wanted to be with you today."

Jake seemed surprised by what I told him. And pleased.

Soon we caught up with the others. They were turned for our arrival and seemed to be expecting me to say something more. Not wanting to disappoint them, I ventured, "When you meet a new person, it's real important you find out what he knows and can do. It might be helpful to you."

I continued, "See that lean-to over there? Since Ben and his Dad built it earlier this week, everybody on the beach has crawled into it. You can, too. You could even decide to build a new and better one together.

"Did you notice that Ben's carrying two masks and a snorkel? And here's a raft for surf riding. I'll be blowing it up shortly. Ben enjoys sharing his things, and he *just might* do that with you. You never know!"

They seemed interested, and, by silent agreement, went together with him toward the pounding surf. Dad, who had been watching curiously at a distance, came to me inquiring what had happened. Once caught up, he decided to wade in and supervise the action. All went well.

As time went by, Dad and Ben wandered further down the beach to catch some bigger waves. The youngsters playing in front of me gathered to return home. But first they approached the blanket where I sat cross-stitching.

"We need to leave now. We tried to tell Ben and shouted for him, but he's too far away and can't hear us." They seemed almost apologetic. "Would you please tell him for us?"

"I'll be sure to do that for you," I promised.

As they sauntered homeward, Jake broke away and came running back to my chair. "*Please* make sure to tell Ben?" he pleaded.

"You can count on me, Honey," I asserted. "And, Jake?" I continued. "I'm real proud of you guys."

He grinned and suddenly squared his small shoulders, then tore off to rejoin the others.

When Ben returned with his Dad, I told him. He absorbed the message with a new sense of self-importance.

Later that afternoon, after we'd eaten our dinner, we heard voices outside the trailer. It was Ben's new-found friends.

"Can Ben come out and play 'Capture The Flag?'" they wanted to know. Of course, he could.

The joyful sounds that now came from *all* the children of the campground filled those who heard with quiet gratitude.

Two hours later, when mosquitos became avenging hordes and dampness frosted hair and lashes, Ben came home to the safety of our patio netting.

As he sat on the same couch he'd earlier occupied in a state of abject discouragement, he reviewed the day with happy exhaustion.

"Did you learn anything today, Ben?" I asked, grinning.

"Yep. I found out that sometimes I don't need to be afraid of bullies. They probably don't know any more than I do, might not have any new or better ideas, and can't do some of the things I can do!" He thought some more. "It was a fun day, Mom. Thanks."

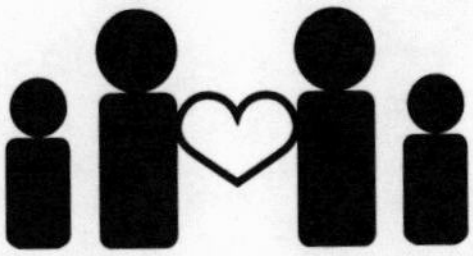

We're Scared of Teens

OW CAN you work with adolescents? They're impossible!" Those who work in our agency get asked this question from incredulous adults all the time. Teens are scary to grown-ups. News reports are filled with horror stories of youth gangs perpetrating violence and larceny in every community. And we fear the same is likely to happen in ours unless we stay vigilant.

I remember when I was scared to death of them. Hired to teach math at a local high school, I faced a classroom of strangely dressed and coifed, slumped, frowning adolescent bodies looking for all the world like they were determined to do absolutely nothing I might ask of them.

"How do you get them to do what you want?" A competent medical professional encountering her first onslaught of teens was bemoaning her inability to get them to follow her health-critical directives.

This frustration gets to us adults. Why doesn't just *telling them* produce action? Why are these young people so downright obstinate when it comes to taking directions from us? Don't we, after all, know better what's good for them? Why must they buck us in our best efforts to help them?

"These teen moms," spoke a referring professional, "can't you get them to just clean up their babies and put proper clothes on them, and feed themselves well and keep their apartments spotless?"

How can we expect cleanliness from persons who've been told in their growing-up years that they're sloppy, messy, dirty, disorganized, useless, incompetent, lazy and rude?

They've heard that they don't really know anything and can't do anything right, and now that they "made their beds" they should sleep in them.

Do these kinds of put-downs ever produce good behavior in young people? No. Instead, the young discouraged either live up or down to those bad things they've been told they are. Some, on the other hand, who try to make good of their situations find the climb out of the hole they've been dumped into almost insurmountable.

What kind of adult attitude helps young people build productive, hopeful, responsible lives, one that looks beyond the tired, discouraged, shamed faces and sees something else? To adopt it, we must transform our vision so we can see that beyond the facade there frequently live caring, loving, responsible, striving spirits waiting for the chance to do the best they can.

Then, we must land on the small things they do which are sterling. We build on what we've seen in them. We rejoice.

That's what teens are looking for – adults who live with the vision of who they really are. They trust that someone out there will look past the clothes, the hair draped to hide faces, the slump that says, "I'm no good, and I'll prove it to you." They're looking for grown-ups with insight, adults who'll declare with absolute certainty, "I know who you *really* are, and I expect you'll rise to the very best."

They hope for the chance to do better by their loved ones than was done by them. It's an idealized picture of the way life should be lived. Often it's magic they expect to happen, and soon. But first they hang out awhile. There's lots of time.

They look for the adult who can stand by them, someone who listens well and can be consulted for advice and counsel. And the adult they seek must understand, should the young person "screw up," that love and respect must never be withdrawn. Too many teens have learned that "messing up" results in losing adult love.

They also look for someone to trust them, just to give them a chance. From their experience, they know that being a teen means you're guilty. Of what? … of whatever it is that adults fear most: vandalism, shop-lifting, assault, rudeness, unbridled energy, loss of control, speaking one's mind, taking on the establishment – anything!

Not long ago, a shopkeeper looking for temporary clerks shared his own version of this terror. Three teens came in to ask about employment. Only one spoke up, so the entrepreneur gave out only one form. Not knowing why they had come three-strong, he became brusque, anxious and irritable. What they read from him was rudeness and hostility. Anger rose up in their spirits, and any hope of employment they'd had upon entering the store crashed down around them.

Why did they come in as three? Because *they* were scared, too. Moral support prompted his two friends to accompany the third young man; he felt he couldn't ask for the application without the support of their presence.

Had the poor man known at the time how scared they were, he would have smiled to himself, been cordial and confident with them and encouraged them to talk about how hard it was to find work. He might even have given them some helpful advice on how to inquire about work without scaring potential bosses half to death.

Teens need adults to gently correct them, not scold or put them down, but *correct* them. To do this adults need to be specific about the expectation of good behavior. It could sound like this:

"When you need a job application, go into a shop alone. Have your friends wait out of sight in another place. A whole group of teens can be scary to adults. Grown-ups don't know what you'll do. Dress well, be clean, speak respectfully. You'll make a better impression and will more likely land a job."

Teens need adults to extend them respect, to treat them as worthy individuals.

A fine older man I know who is remarkably successful with troubled young people uses this opener when he first meets them:

"I will attempt to *earn* your respect, but I will never fail to *give* you respect ... regardless what you've done."

Teens can smell adult fear, but they read it as hostility. We need to understand that teens are as afraid of us as we are of them. We have to make the first move. We must reach out with confidence to them. We must believe in them and like them. We must expect that their best selves will respond to our respectfulness, and that rapport will follow.

Only with these in place will we be able to understand, advise, comfort, help, enjoy them and extend them our wisdom. And we'll see a new humanness, a softness now missing from our interactions with them, come forth into both our lives.

Partying Teens

IN MOST STATES, teens may not legally use alcohol until the age of 21. If they violate this injunction at our hands or in our homes, we are responsible for the consequences. Whether we are home at the time is immaterial. What happens in our absence is still in our hands, and we need to face this as our adolescents move into the party scene.

"But the kids won't go to parties that are chaperoned!" I hear from countless parents of adolescents. Something's wrong. I wonder if we've bought into the "cool parent" myth. It tells us to face certain incontrovertible realities: that our teens are drinking alcohol, that they want to be alone at their parties, and that we're old fashioned if we insist on being present at their get-togethers.

The bare-faced reality, though, is this: they are not yet adults. Despite their grown-up appearance and mature abilities, teens are still children. They still look to us as models and guides. Standing up for the very best codes of behavior is still our job; they need this from us. They watch what we do and take their cues as they interpret our actions.

If they hear us say they shouldn't drink or use drugs, then they expect we'll follow suit. If we use alcohol in our homes, do we serve it in the context of family and celebration and food? Is it used with appropriateness and in balance and with moderation? Do we instruct and model the proper use of this substance? Do we caution and warn of abuse? Are we open to self-examination and criticism of our own drinking? Is there a history of drinking problems in our families? Are we sharing this with our youngsters, cautioning that heredity is a common factor in perpetuating this disease?

Some parents say, "Oh, we take their keys when they come for parties. That way we can be sure that designated drivers are liquor-free and that no one who leaves here drunk is also driving." Such a policy ignores the fact that we are violating the law by allowing teens to drink in our homes. We have no control over who drives once the group has left our premises. Serving minors still makes us culpable before the law.

"But we trust them," I hear parents say as they leave their child's house party. It's not a matter of trust. When peers attend a party, the adolescent host is put into an awfully awkward situation: he or she must now assume authority over those from whom he or she also seeks approval. They are all of the same approximate age, and they can exert enormous pressure on one another. Teens desperately need to belong, to be close, to develop their own social identity. Putting them into a policing role is potential peer group suicide. Adults must have the guts to assume this role; it's appropriately theirs, regardless of its unpopularity.

Unchaperoned teen parties have the potential of irrevocably damaging our children's lives. I know young women who have gotten pregnant at such events; I have met the grieving parents of teens killed from the alcohol served at them; I have visited host homes torn apart as if pillaged by war.

We can't allow this kind of destruction to happen in our homes. We are parents first, not buddies, to our young people. Unless we dare to take supervisory measures during our youngsters' growing-up years, we cannot insure their physical safety, their emotional well-being, their abstinence from addictive substances, or their eventual entry into adulthood.

A challenge and a plea: let's have no more unsupervised teen parties and no alcohol and no drugs. Let's show by example what we expect of them. Let's be there for our children with courage and strength and caring.

Chaperoning, Some Tips

CHAPERONING A TEEN PARTY is an art form. Parents somehow need to balance the energy and the fun parties generate with their sense of responsibility for keeping everyone safe. It's a partnership that begins in the planning stages and continues through to final mop-up. Young people must know we trust them; they must also understand that we will be there for them should trouble arise.

Here are some suggestions others have found helpful in overseeing teen parties.

- As soon as possible after the idea has been hatched, adults and teens need to sit together and plan. What type of party will it be? Who and how many will be invited? What kinds of foods and beverages will be most appealing? Which days and hours are best?
- The young people must then follow through with clear invitations, food shopping and preparation, house arrangements and decorating, and cost contributions. They'll quickly learn that hosting successful get-togethers involves more than meets the eye.
- Rules of partying should come next. Under no circumstances can alcohol or drugs be allowed on the premises. If this directive gets out well ahead of the party, no one will be embarrassed arriving with forbidden substances.
- Close neighbors should be apprised. Parking arrangements can be negotiated and acceptable noise levels guaranteed. Our home is often filled with music, and we are, therefore, sensitive to areas of our house that "leak" sound to nearest neighbors. Windows can be closed, sound-proofing installed, drapes drawn, etc.
- To help with supervision the night of the party, parents might invite another couple or two for company. While adults visit with

one another nearby, the young people can feel their support and stand-by readiness should trouble break out.

- One couple encourages the party go-ers to sign in with erasable markers on the front of their refrigerator. This helps adults to properly receive and transmit telephone messages and to acquaint themselves with the names of their children's friends.

- Parties often precipitate "crashers." If the host or hostess doesn't know these youngsters or has no desire to have them attend, the chaperons can turn them away without placing the burden of policing on teen shoulders. Picture two older, adult men refusing entry to the uninvited. Discouraging potential unpleasantness is always preferable to breaking up trouble once it has already begun.

- As much as is possible, the teens need to be given their own party place in the house so that they can talk freely and enjoy one another without constant adult oversight. Many parents seem to have a fine-honed sixth sense about youthful activity in their home; this they should use to prompt unexpected apparitions at the party. While presenting a confident assurance that, of course, all is well, they can at the same time keep party behavior standards high. Refilling trays of goodies, replacing beverages, appreciating new musical sounds … opportunities for surprise appearances are many.

- As the party draws to a close, chaperones might issue a "warning shot" to the teen host or hostess. When young people prepare to leave, adults can commend them on their good humor and cooperation; they can invite them to return, modeling gracious hospitality to their teens.

- Cleanup. Each family has a different tradition. Ours is this: Before bedtime, the house must be restored to its former state. We all help out, and it often becomes the springboard for "debriefing" which has transpired during the evening. There's usually a "high" buried in the fatigue that is best appreciated by those who are part of it.

Teen parties are an occasion for shared growing-up. Learning the fine art of hospitality is important to our young. It's learned best in a trusting, warm place ... home.

Time for a Laughter Break

A DARK SHAPE SKITTERED across the road. My right foot leaped to the brake. Nearing the creature, I saw it was only a plastic garbage bag being blown erratically by the wind. It had looked for all the world to me like an animal lumbering across the road from woods to woods.

"You need a bumper sticker," my husband commented.

"Wha …?" I knew how he objected to these.

"Caution: I brake for plastic bags!" he filled in the blank he had so expertly set up.

Despite my early morning fog, I laughed … and laughed … and laughed. It felt good, and I clung to it longer than I would have expected.

It's what we need – laughter. More of it than we seem to be generating in our day-to-day.

OUR LITTLE BEN came to me the other day with that famous Abbott and Costello trick of adding up seven twelves and arriving at 21. He had mastered not only how to add them (defying all laws of place value) but also how to prove his addition by dividing the 21 incorrectly by seven to get 12.

It was breaking him up. Soon we were both in pieces.

A child laughs this hard only when he feels he's pulled a fast one on the rules that silly old adults fastidiously create. We laughed right alongside.

Mischief. It comes readily when the absurdity of one's life brings it forth. I feel deeply that we can't live very long in the tightness brought on by life's circumstances, that there's something in us wanting to break out and be just as absurd as these endless trials.

"I'm going to find some trouble I can get into!" I spoke con-spiratorially to a friend at church. "This is no place to plot mis-chief," my quiet and conservative adult self warned.

"So what! I won't hurt anyone ... promise." The giggle started deep down and rose like champagne. Who can resist its magic pull? Just because our hair is graying and our wrinkles happen to be setting in a bit (prematurely, may I add?) doesn't mean we can't turn things upside down from time to time.

Do the unexpected. Try a twist on the usual, a turnabout you've been dying to do. Serve cake for dinner ... nothing else, just cake. Nobody'll die. They might hesitate a bit at first, cautious, won-dering whether or not to be worried about the cook. Once they catch on, though, they'll be fine. Trust me.

Or, try renting a funny video instead of snoozing before the T V sitcoms. It's hard nowadays to find one that isn't violent or risque or perverse. I run the risk of getting depressed whenever I enter the video store. V H S covers loom dark with gleaming weapons, sweaty bodies, tantalizingly abbreviated garments, or ghoulish nightmares.

I turn away. It's the funny ones I seek. They can inevitably be found on white backgrounds with silly-looking individuals doing weird things ... or animals looking more intelligent than the humans. And they're labeled P G , P G -13, or just plain G . Harm-less. But sometimes awful, too.

"Beethoven," "Straight Talk," "Sister Act", "Money Pit" ... good ones live on those shelves, too. Worth an evening of gut laughter.

"You're escaping!" my young friend objected.

"Yes, yes, yes, yes!" I shout. "Hallelujah! You're absolutely right!" And why not? For a moment. Our spirits need light and joy. Our stomach muscles need exercise. We need to sleep a bit more peacefully having released the stresses with laughter.

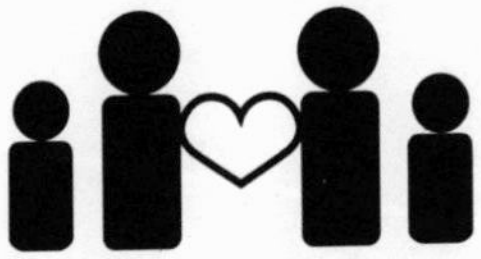

Taking Time

THE DAY WAS CRISP and sunny. Tourists strolled along the waterfront; they sat watching ocean waves lapping the shore; they waited in lines for refreshments; they stood in lines for tours leaving regularly from crowded docks. The scene was peaceful and festive.

With his back to the shore, a man was seen standing a short distance from the promenade. In his mid-thirties, he busily fed coins into the public phone while his wiggly toddler amused himself from his perch on dad's back. The father made call after call, left message after message for absent business associates, finalized product delivery details, placed orders for new shipments and dictated instructions to office staff.

It all seemed a bit odd to those sitting nearby; his activity had already continued for some time. By now, the youngster was attempting to get his dad's attention. His whining could be heard above the businesslike adult voice. In no uncertain terms, the father expressed his annoyance, and the little boy began looking very unhappy.

Soon a young woman with her 3-year-old in tow could be seen briskly heading toward the caller. She looked angry, impatient, hurt. Her opening words rebuked him so sharply that onlookers could hear each one. Why hadn't he finished his business? The tour boat would be leaving soon, and they'd miss it. Did she want him to return to the office instead, he snapped back. As if suddenly conscious that they were attracting an audience, the couple hushed their conversation, and the young mother retreated to the waiting boat lines.

By the time the businessman-father had completed his calls and walked to the dock, he saw that the tour boat had already left its pier. The young woman looked heartbroken. She stood silent and dejected beside him.

The husband/father had chosen to make phone calls instead of memories. And his decision had made all the difference to his family. His chance was gone; so was theirs.

My mom has a saying: "The work will always be there waiting for you. It's not a rabbit. It won't run away." She'd use it when she saw one of us torn by indecision: whether to do our "duty" or that one-in-a-million "together" thing. She always encouraged us to choose the latter, and she was right.

A DAD STOPPED by his neighbor's house not long ago. He chatted about his work. It seemed like he was away every week-end training guard troops.

"You must miss not being with your family," said the empathetic hostess.

"Oh, no! I get Tuesdays and Wednesdays off, instead. This gives me a chance to go off hunting or fishing by myself. No one's around, and I love it!"

Nearby, his son tugged at his shirt. "Can't we go now, Dad? You promised we'd play toss and catch at the field." Reluctantly, the father followed his son as he raced ahead of him toward the end of the road.

THE YOUNG GRANDSON stood weeping, trying to compose himself. Mourners gathered around him at the grave site.

"He was the finest man I ever knew," he began. "He took me to work with him when he laid bricks. He was the best bricklay-er around, you know." He paused. "He'd pick us grandkids up and take us out in his truck and tell us we were the best grandkids in the whole world. And he'd buy us ice cream or popsicles or candy bars. We used to look forward to Saturdays."

LOVE IS MEMORIES: Time spent together and loving it.

The Family in the Work Place

He'll be gone again all of next week. It's awful. And my single friends don't help at all. They either shrug their shoulders, not understanding, or they tell me I ought to 'buck up,' hang in there, shoulder my burden." It was a young mother telling of her isolation during the frequent and lengthy business trips her husband needed to take as part of his job.

Alone. Our young parents are asked to raise their children, in many circumstances, alone. Often the work place puts the lion's share of overtime and extensive travel on its younger employees. This leaves the primary caregiver with little support.

When the tired spouse returns home late on Friday night, he or she dumps frustration with the suitcase and tries to recover during the short weekend before the next trip begins.

New behavioral rules based on situations that occurred during the week don't get communicated, and, without fail, arguments between adults ensue. The absent parent feels powerless in contributing anything but occasional entertainment to the children's upbringing and can soon lose touch with the young ones.

Multiplied by several years, this regimen can bankrupt the relationships of the absent parent with his or her spouse and with the children. All the closeness, camaraderie, school activity and educational support has been missed; these times are impossible to recapture. They're gone.

And there's another process that happens: An emotional distance grows between the parents attempting to cope with this trap. They find it hard to stay close. Their gulf widens, and by the time children reach adolescence, the adults are so distant other that they begin shouting just to heard.

"They'd rather give the children $10 than 10 minutes," complained an experienced juvenile officer from a local police department. "Parents do it to them. It's *adults* who create troubled children."

Having to choose money or career advancement over investing time with growing children is a frightening thought. The choice isn't always a clear one; it seldom pops right out at working parents. Instead, they see that jobs are dear, that the economy is insecure. Responsible parents must provide for their family's basic needs; after all, everybody's got to survive.

In questioning company policy from a variety of area businesses, I discovered that none had formal policies that spelled out how that company supported its employees in their family needs. Most agreed that allowances were individually granted and dependent upon particular supervisors.

The most enlightened company posture I found extended to its employees the same "customer-first" policy as it applied to its business clients. It felt that, if management treated its workers and their basic needs first, the company's products and services would also get better. So far, this philosophy has proven out.

Families today need more support and encouragement than ever before. Because they rely on the marketplace for supplying basic needs, they also feel they can commit significant amounts of their time making it work. In turn, they expect that the work place should commit to supporting a whole-person employee management strategy.

Employees come from families. They emerge from them as they start for work. They return to them when their work is done. They keep coming day after day because they love their families and want to provide well for them. Ignoring this reality, pretending work is their only existence, belies the facts. But integrating this reality into the work place invites a humanness, a gentleness, a productivity quotient that can only bring a greater prosperity and excellence to all involved.

The Value of Work

WORKING IS what we do for the biggest part of our lives. The label "workaholic" is like the label "perfectionist" to those who hear it: it's either loved or hated, depending on who's doing the talking.

We work, and we teach children to work. How?

First, by what we *do* when we do what we call "work." The children watch from the sidelines.

They see us do our "turn down" on Sunday nights as we become increasingly aware that Monday morning is around the corner.

They hear our alarms blare us into our early morning consciousness.

They cringe at the sound of our craggy voices cutting through the early fog, barking commands, groping for the bathroom light, sighing as the hot, spray hits our half-asleep bodies.

They know how desperately we reach for the steaming cup of black coffee. They ultimately relax as they watch the first caustic gulps slide down our throats.

Work. Something we appear to dread, a necessary evil that must be endured if we are to bring bread to our tables.

Is this the only picture we project onto our youngsters? Do they ever see us in action once we've arrived at the work place? If they could see us there, what would they carry away with them? Would they suddenly comprehend the meaning of what we do and why? Might we consider taking them with us one day?

Way back in the '60s a study was done on the nature of work. I don't remember a lot of the findings, but I've never forgotten two pieces: The top motivator among all types of labor studied was growth potential. The second motivator was work satisfaction.

Salary, benefits, environment, hours – all those factors about which we usually care so deeply before taking on a work commitment – fell far behind the first two.

How do we translate these realizations into our home lives? Is there something we can do to help our children learn about work as a positive and productive process, not just as something we all have to do if we're to survive?

In the most profoundly realistic sense, we can see ourselves and those we love as gifted. The recognition and acknowledgment of personal talents brings with it the understanding that each of us has a specific mission: to grow our gifts and to share them with others.

Indeed, the growing of talents is bound to the sharing of them.

This requires a mind shift. Instead of seeing our gifts as given for our own satisfaction, and enjoyment and fame, we might dedicate the growing of these toward contributing to and raising the quality of our community's life.

For example, we all work in the home because taking care of this environment improves total family functioning. We prepare food for nourishment and aesthetic enjoyment and social interaction.

We clean and repair and make beds and shovel snow and vacuum and do laundry and water plants and straighten pile-ups so there'll be order and so that residents can move about safely and can entertain friends and can relax and be healthy.

Some of our family members are better at particular tasks than others; some don't mind doing what others dread. Each has a preference or developed expertise. Smart managers, the parents-in-residence, allow and encourage family members to specialize.

"First comes the work, then the play" presents a good maxim but needn't make the doing of it drudgery. Putting lively, "up" music on the stereo, concocting games around beating rugs or moving furniture or dusting these have been known to accelerate clock time.

Setting aside, say, Saturday mornings as whole-family cleanup times also helps. "Put them all in the same boat," another good maxim, rounds out the directives for teaching good work habits.

Don't pay for work children do in the home. You don't get paid and shouldn't. The reward is the application of personal giftedness to the common good and a sense of accomplishment at a job well done. Family members learn to work together, to give orders, to take them, to experience satisfaction, to set family goals, to create new things, to get tired together, and to relax and enjoy together.

Work and play can join hands. When our work *is* our play, our fatigue will not harm us. Rather, it will create an energy wellspring that will refresh, enhance and deeply satisfy.

Sick Children

FLU SEASON is murder on both children and parents. We've all been there. The alarm goes off at 6:30 A.M., and Bobby is slow rising. He's whining and generally uncooperative in getting himself washed and dressed and ready for school.

"I don't feel too well, Mom," he mumbles. We wonder how we can tell if he just doesn't want to go to school that day because there's something he dreads, or if he's really and truly starting to do battle with a virus.

Our first temptation, since we're feeling healthy and well, is to say, "You're fine. Just get ready. Have some breakfast and go ahead to school. You'll feel better before you know it."

What's really going through our heads is a monologue: "Golly, this just isn't very convenient today. I've got two important meetings at work, and I need to find a sitter, and I'll have to make an appointment with the doctor and just generally rearrange my life, and he's probably not really sick, anyway."

But what if he is? Remember the time you went to work feeling woozy and weak but convinced yourself it was all in your head? Then, at about 9:30 A.M., you turned gray and everyone in the office asked you why you came in at all?

Not only was that a dumb move, but you also may have exposed your co-workers to your very own personal brand of virus. So you meekly packed up and headed home to nurse your illness with their permission.

Now, back to poor Bobby: You're not sure just how to confirm his condition, and you're not clairvoyant about what will happen next if this is really a flu brewing inside him. So, you decide to collect some data.

First comes the thermometer. For me, a temperature bordering on 100 degrees means something's amiss. Next comes the throat examination cum flashlight. If it looks red when he says "Ahhhhh," or it has little white things on it, I hand him his pillow, put on the vaporizer, and call the physician's answering service. I'm home for the day. Everything else will just have to wait.

Then comes the gland test. Feeling around under his jaw, I look for variations of what I've come to know as normal for the child. If the complaint is a stomach ache, I ask other related questions and offer dry toast or soda crackers or tea; maybe a poached egg, if it sounds like something he might be able to tolerate.

If nothing has turned up yet, I try the "Are you worried about going to school today?" tactic. Then, I listen hard to what he has to say. It's important at this juncture not to start getting judgmental; he might have a legitimate concern that is such a worry that he's actually feeling physically ill. We've all felt it.

Once I'm finished hearing him out, I might want to help him "process" what could be done to solve his problem. My posture is not to be unbelieving but rather supportive and encouraging of whatever it takes to get him back in operation again.

If I've decided to let them try going to school, I should make sure that he has my telephone number and the assurance that I'll be there for him should anything develop.

If I've decided he should stay home, I need to set some strict rules: a doctor's visit, a half-hour of television, lots of liquids and bed rest. There's no running around or playing until the next day, if he's feeling better. Sometimes one day of super care at the start of an illness can avoid many days of severe symptoms.

Dr. T. Berry Brazelton of Boston Children's Hospital speaks tenderly of days gone by when mothers used to show special love to their children at time of illness. "We used to look forward to being sick," he says.

Taken in the context of this situation, perhaps this is a good time to encourage parents to take the extra time and care to help their children at times of illness. Our work places need to support this mothering/fathering effort by helping to facilitate re-scheduling for family needs.

Sickness is something none of us enjoys. But it comes, anyway. So, let's make this occasion one more vehicle in which we show our little ones that they come first, and that we care about helping them get very well, very soon.

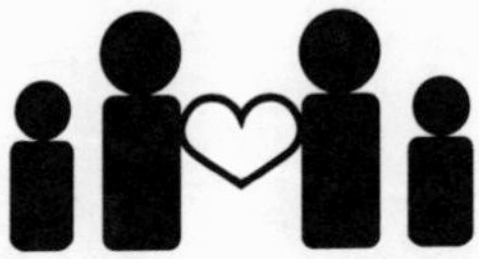

Learning to Fly

We are each angels with one wing. The only way we can fly is by hugging one another." It's a quote I once read that struck hard. It's a lesson that works for couples, for families, for people who care about one another, for anyone in a relationship. It speaks to our incompleteness, to our need for togetherness, to our powerlessness when we stand alone.

A young woman called me recently and spoke of her four-year friendship/dating experience with a young man.

"I don't think we're going anywhere. During the past year, he has done nothing to confront me or challenge me or urge my growth onward. And I can't seem to engage him with my unhappiness or concern. All he wants to do is please me. It drives me mad!"

"Why do you expect conflict in this relationship? Isn't it nice to have peace and contentment and mutual pleasing?" I tried to get at the root of what she thought real love was all about.

"I'm in this to grow. *We're* in this to grow together," she struggled with her meaning. "I expect that if we're going to be a couple we should be committed to helping one another to become better and better. We *need* each other."

Families are sometimes defined as two or more persons in committed relationship with one another. Within them, the individuals live out the love they profess and work toward the completion of one another's growth.

But it doesn't always happen that way.

A young woman married 11 years suddenly found herself with her husband gone.

"He just came home one night and told me he didn't love me anymore and was leaving. I couldn't believe what I was hearing! And then he left, and he won't talk to me any more." She was stunned and confused.

In an effort to comprehend what had happened, she came to talk. I discovered that, although they had been to counseling several times, he had divulged little about his feelings.

"He's terribly nebulous. He's deep, and I have difficulty comprehending him."

I wondered if this was purposeful on his part. Was he being obscure so that she couldn't see inside him? Was this a "studied" evasion of intimacy? She seemed so anxious to get closer, and he seemed to be running away. Then he did, physically.

In order to "fly hugging one another" we must dare to be open to each other. We need to trust enough to risk exposing our faults, admitting we can't make it without the other's loving counsel and encouragement.

But we're all a bit afraid. Each time we face the one we love we must overcome our conviction that we'll get "done in" by that person. That's how most of us have learned to interact with the people we have known in any depth, and also how we've grown up in our families. It's dangerous to be close to another. Why should we trust an individual who knows best where our weaknesses lie and can push all the right buttons?

Love doesn't stay in one place. It is a living, dynamic, changing thing. It's organic. It takes guts to grab hold of it, say "Yes" to it, hang in there when things get rough, remain committed ... not throw it away because it hurts too much to stay open to the other.

In any love, we sometimes need a "third person" to help us really listen to what the other is saying. After several years, we become dulled to the new messages being offered by our partner; we only seem to hear the old ones. They might be filled with pain, and hurt has a way of interfering with messages of the heart.

We're made to fly. We even dream about it. But to fly, we must know more about the fine art of loving one another.

Loving one another takes energy and risk-taking and lots of hugging. The trip has its perils but can't be equalled for its magnificence.

Parable of Relationships

WHY DO THEY all gather on our bed? It seems to be the place they can talk about heart things, wondering if life should be as it is, stretching to understand its mysteries. The children *all* do it when they return home. It's like they never left.

Their topics are as grown-up as they are. That night, the subject was relationships: commitments, marriage, intimacy. Their faces showed an intense involvement, a profound need to grasp the realities and principles simmering beneath the surface of their experiences.

"Why don't they just talk it out?" one of them addressed a puzzling isolation she observed in a married couple recently observed. "That's what we do. That's the only way to do it. It only makes sense!"

I saw the earnestness, the vehemence. Her spirit was frustrated, youthful and energetic. Why hadn't the couple managed its relationship with the forthrightness she practiced so clearly?

"Life has a way of stockpiling hurts and injuries that make straight-talking nearly impossible for some," I tried to explain.

Her puzzled look told me she wanted more. It wasn't clear.

"Shall I tell you a story?" I asked.

"Oh, yes. Please."

TWO YOUNG lovers pledged their troth and celebrated their joy. Everyone came and spoke of the great love they shared. The world was at their feet, and dreams flowed like abundant streams around them.

Soon they realized that their love needed to make a home. So they searched far and wide hoping to find just the right one. Their efforts were soon rewarded. They discovered a beautiful old Victorian house on a large parcel of land and consisting of many, many rooms. It had two stories, an attic, a widow's peak and lovely, generous spaces into which their love would grow. Here they could raise a family.

They moved in and carefully began the task of making each corner cozy, warm, and welcoming ... until they got to that remote room at the end of the second-floor hallway. It was too small to hold a bed or dresser. They argued and disagreed and finally came to an impasse. Whenever either of them mentioned it again the other turned away or scowled or looked hurt.

Before long, neither would utter a word concerning that tiny space. The rest of their lives were so rich and happy that bringing up their Waterloo seemed pointless. Besides, if mentioning it created hurt, there was no purpose to it. Soon the room ceased to exist. They not only avoided talking about it, they went so far as to lock it and store the key in a jar on a high kitchen shelf.

As the years went by they found themselves closing other rooms, locking them, and storing the keys in that same jar. One room was abandoned over the issue of money ... how to spend it and whether or not they had enough to do with it what they wanted.

Another room was sealed because it used to be where Grandma stayed. The thought of seeing it again hurt them so much they entombed it.

Before long, every room on the second floor was closed. Nobody ever bothered going up there anymore. It was so cold and empty and lonely. Shades were drawn, windows streaked with ancient dust, spring housecleaning abandoned ... even family members were scared to walk its corridors.

When children asked what lay behind the locked doors, they were told it was nothing, that certain hurtful memories had prompted them to have been shut years ago. Soon the young ones grew up and left and no one asked anymore.

But the house kept getting smaller. The couple missed their children, and so they decided to close the family room. Because they hadn't entertained in a long time, they shut the living room as well. Their dinnertimes echoed their silences–'had for years now. Why not drape the china closet and furniture ... and put the silver away, and the linen?

Soon, only the kitchen was left. A hot cup of coffee and the morning paper still satisfied. Sometimes the two of them would even cook a meal together. They did still enjoy doing that. And it was safe: Arguments seldom happened there. Once in awhile they even shared some laughter during dish duty.

They lived this way until the morning they got news of his layoff. The kitchen telephone rang; it was his boss calling from work. The job he'd held for years had been cut. He wasn't needed anymore.

A new sadness crept into their shrunken world, and it drew them further apart. So they closed the kitchen, too.

As they sat on the front stoop, they gazed plaintively at each other. They began wondering what had happened to their nice warm house. What had brought them out into the cold?

They'd had such dreams, once. Where had they gone? Why had they not done the things they'd planned?

But, they were tired now ... and discouraged. No fresh hopes kindled their spirits, no plans, no fun or mischief or gaiety ... only the sky overhead.

"Their home!" she cried. "They still have their home! Can't they open it up again and clean out the rooms and decorate and have a housewarming and face the sorrows and tragedies they've put away for so long?"

"Yes, Honey, they can. But it's been years of running away and hiding and avoiding. It'll take a lot of hard work to do this, and maybe some good help and support." I loved the young face so hopefully struggling before me.

"Why don't they go back, match the keys to the right rooms, and one by one unlock them?" she persisted.

"Only if they remember the love they bore one another can they do this," I spoke in a whisper, "and take each other's hands, open the forbidden doors, and with great faith walk through the memories. Someone needs to pick up the broom, someone the dustpan; the drapes must be opened to the sunshine and the windows scrubbed clean."

They'll need some help. But I hope they'll try. Some good years remain, and they deserve the joy.

Try Forgiveness

THEY SEEM always to be in conflict. Their marriage is one of some longstanding, and it is clear to any who know them that there have been many hurts along the way.

They are both bright, and neither has ever forgotten a one of those battles. Both can recite chapter and verse of each conflict in the most minute detail. The only difference between their stories is the speaker's point of view; each story has a winner and a loser.

Whenever irritability surfaces between them, one or the other feels free to interject a well-executed jab from a well-recalled past. It's delivered as a sarcastic remark, a scathing judgment or a prediction about what the spouse will do this time based on prior mistakes. Watching from a safe distance, onlookers are embarrassed and wonder about the role they should play. Most cut their visits short and slink quietly away, making excuses about needing to be elsewhere.

I recently found myself in this position but had no ready means of escape. Sensing my discomfort, the wife turned to me and asked in desperation, "What's wrong with us? Why can't we seem to get along with any degree of peace between us?"

I mumbled something about competing with one another, but my observation fell on deaf ears. She couldn't see what I saw, and I felt no need to argue or insist. It seemed that more conflict wasn't the tonic required in this situation.

Weeks later I found myself looking over a display of reduced books in a local store I haunt. When my eyes rested on "The Forgiving Marriage", I started.

I had an instant sense of recognition: That was the thought I had failed to generate when my friend and I were talking about their relationship.

It was so obvious. Anyone who's been committed in a relationship for any length of time knows how many possibilities for psychic injury can present themselves. Once the damage is done, it can't be undone. It begins to fester, only to be spewed out when one side or another can gain strategic advantage from it.

Somehow the past has to be put away, apology must be made for hurts inflicted, whether or not intended, and forgiveness has to be showered upon the individual whom we count as having damaged us. Both have to participate, and the forgiveness must flow in two directions.

How truly possible is this? Under what circumstances? When would it be the most safe to implement? Shouldn't there be certain basic understandings already in place between the individuals involved before attempting something so risky? And shouldn't each person have felt the reality of forgiveness from having known it in his/her own life? What can and should be forgiven? Is there anything that can't be?

Should a mediator acceptable to both parties be present to help the process, or is it intensely private? Is it possible for partners to re-extend trust to each other so that repair can happen? Might greater damage occur as a result of forgiving? Should boundaries be set ahead of time? The questions come endlessly, but my spirit leaps at the possibilities it engenders.

I bought the book and then wondered how I would get it to her. When I called that night to tell her of my find, I also confessed that forgiveness was a thought I wish I'd had when we'd spoken about their marriage earlier.

"Do you want me to check the book out for you?" she offered, "It sounds like something I'd like to read." Had she witnessed my awe-struck reaction, she would have giggled.

"You guessed it!" I replied. "I'll put it in the mail tomorrow."

She obviously forgave me for reopening the difficult subject. She also accepted my humble offering. I had the feeling there'd been forgiveness given and received right there on the phone.

I guess the message here is simple: Try forgiveness. When we keep revisiting the same old hurts, those about which we can do nothing, we have little to lose by forgiving others ... and ourselves, too.

The process engages us in attempting to comprehend one another. Deborah Tannen's book "You Just Don't Understand" declares that men and women continually misinterpret one another's communications. It's not just us; it's everybody! So, we can roll up our sleeves and start going at it.

We grew up with "Forgive and forget," and sneer our cynicism, "You want me to get a lobotomy?" But do this we must. Once we accept another's genuine apology, we must put the old hurt away. Erase it. Don't fight with it any more. The time for wrestling is before forgiving, not after.

It's hard, this process of forgiving, but worth it. It humbles, it makes us accountable for caring about our relationships, and it calls us to change ourselves.

Couple Time

Important things take time. People are the most important "things" in our lives. But do we give them our best, planned, prime, committed time? Or do we just give those people we most love our leftovers?

And, now that we're looking at all of this, who on our list gets our uninterrupted time? Is it our co-workers, those we serve, our children, our parents or in-laws, our closest friends? Which of them must wait their turn? How do we decide who gets our time?

Who's first on our "important people" list? Society tells us that children come first. They don't. Our "coupleness" does.

Many years ago, my husband and I bought the first message, that children are at the center of our relationship. We proceeded nobly living out its dire consequences: we drew farther and farther apart. Our marriage foundered and plunged into crisis.

Suddenly we realized that we had to re-center our attentions and rediscover our core: one another. It was our love that had generated the other pieces of our lives. Our love was unique, and we had lost it. We might even have thrown it away, unknowingly. And now we struggled to get it back. The work was hard, and it was many years overdue.

Recently, I attended a wedding during which the pastor gave gifts to the bride and groom just before they spoke their vows. He them golf balls! His message to them, both golfers, was that they needed to continue spending time with each other and not get lost in individual pursuits that would pull them apart. Then he spoke of the twin wine goblets that they'd receive later, a reminder of the quality moments they were to maintain in their married life.

Researchers who have studied stress in families target insuffi-
cient couple time as one of the top 10 stressors named by both
men and women. This implies that, when a husband and wife care
enough to take time with one another, they help the entire family to better manage stress in daily life. The kind of intimacy that
comes from frequent and sustained communications binds a family together and models a collaborative spirit and energy that
graces our children.

Whenever I suggest that a couple spend special, undivided time
together, I get either puzzled looks or a, "Well, we already do!"
So I explain. Going grocery shopping, attending a movie, partying
with friends, watching TV together, or even doing yardwork with
one another doesn't cut it. The kind of time I'm talking about is
eyeball-to-eyeball, only-you time when each spouse really listens
hard to the other, listens with heart and mind. It's active, interac-
tive, energetic time, not "vegging out" time during which someone or something else does the work.

Picture this. You and your spouse are seated at a candlelit table
with flowers and wine. Others are waiting on you. No telephones
ring, no one approaches with messages, no children or family
members or people from work interrupt the flow. There's nothing
to distract you from one another.

"But what if I can't think of anything to say to him!" a young
wife panicked at the thought.

"Sit there until something comes out of your mouth!" I said, "It's
time you start finding out who he is and who you are again,
before it's too late."

Begin the slow, painful process of re-establishing your relationship — it'll save your family.

What, then, are the guidelines for making sure the time you create for you and your spouse's "couple time" is sufficiently special
and precious? (I'll bet you were good at this when you were dating!)

It must be time away from your home; it must involve only you and your "date," your spouse; it must not involve doing something else, a task, such as shopping, cooking, walking, watching a movie, etc.; it should happen in a public place (so that if you find yourselves arguing, you'll keep it somewhat contained.) but be secluded enough to give you the privacy you require. It doesn't have to cost a lot or be fancy; some couples I know simply enjoy a cup of coffee together. It should last no less than one hour, preferably two or more. It should be a set day of the week *every week*, and the entire world should know you're not available then.

We love going out on Friday nights. There's something wonderful about dumping all the garbage from our work week first. Then, we start getting into the "us" part; conversation is never a problem.

So, put a babysitter on retainer for every Friday or Saturday night, decide where you'd like to go, what your budget will allow, tell the kids it's your "date" night, get all dolled up, bring home a flower for your love, (wives, too!) and discover again the precious person you married.

To My Very Dear Children

YOU HAVE *come to me with a frightening question, "How will I know when I have met my love?" I risk answering it because of my faith in your ability to listen and truly hear not only my words, but also those within your own spirits.*

You must understand that my own wisdom is limited by age, experience and intellect. But I love you and feel you have asked genuinely and urgently for my response.

Please read with care and search your own hearts for the answer you seek. Ultimately, your spirits will be assured when that relationship enters your lives. You'll know with certainty then what you just ponder now.

When I was a college student, I heard from a beloved professor her answer. "When a young woman comes to me saying she's in love, I ask why she loves him. If she is able to tell me, I know right away she's not in love." We puzzled over this, and some understood. Others of us have discovered in time the wisdom of what she told us.

Love is a mystery. It is irrational, sometimes foolish; it doesn't always make sense. It often takes us by surprise. It seldom fits into our plans; indeed, it frequently upsets them. It defies explanation but is sure and confident.

It is not afraid. It sees in the face of the other a kind of mirror. It dares to translate the truth of the other; it sees kindly but gently what lies beneath the other and transforms it into a valued, precious wholeness. Rather than blindness, I think love is a prized vision that sees beyond to the core of the other.

It is trust. It is sincere. It doesn't hide in game-playing and secrecy. It dares to challenge and risk with the assurance that it will survive even the harshest reality. It clarifies and shares burdens, knowing that all will be well if truth rests in its center.

It recognizes that it is not good for us to be alone, that we need to walk side by side with another in partnership. We rejoice in the other's giftedness and feel no need to control or take over and "fix" what the other has done.

Love energizes. It creates. It generates dreams and possibilities. It incorporates differences; it dares to change; it finds the new and untried.

Love is the spark of community-building. Grounded in friendship and hope, it overflows, taking others with it. It is not exclusive, but draws others to it. It seeks to share itself, not to its own diminishment but rather to its growing richness and extension.

And for its two participants it bestows support, comfort and forgiveness. It gives fundamentally of each other's energies without keeping score. It listens with the heart and challenges with truth. It's strong as steel and gentle as rain. It nurtures, cares, holds back the hurt, takes responsibility, and works hard to understand.

It exalts in the other's growth. It risks the unknown with the certainty that love transcends extraordinary upheavals. It does not imprison; it liberates.

Love is everything.

We wish it for you with all our strength. When you find it, tell us, won't you? We'll dance with you and celebrate and embrace the two of you, for you've found the greatest gift of all.

Your always loving,

Mom

Engagement

WE'RE GETTING MARRIED," his voice was quiet and gentle, "I gave her the ring." Our son has grown to love a fine young woman, has spent great energy in developing this dear relationship, and with her has decided to spend a lifetime together.

I wasn't ready for my response to their announcement. They're our first "family marriage"; he's our firstborn; she's his "other." They fit. They work hard on loving each other honestly and openly. They risk arguing – with the courage they'll need to make it through the hard times. All this I have seen, and my eyes well up.

"We hope our marriage will be like yours," she spoke earnestly.

Feeling as though she couldn't possibly be seeing all the warts and wrinkles we'd grown over the past 25 years, I didn't know what to say.

"Are you ready for lots of hard work?" It was all I could muster.

"We're already doing it," she said.

"I have seen you." Indeed I had.

What lay ahead for them? I prayed.

Others have spoken to me of their feelings at receiving marriage announcements from their children.

"He worships the ground she walks on," mom spoke of her future son-in-law. "He also thinks I'm the world's greatest cook. What more can you ask?"

I thought a moment, "Not much...."

Another mother put it this way, "She's awfully good for our son. He's doing things now we never dreamt he'd do. He's 'nesting,' and it suits him well."

Adjustments lie ahead.

We must get together with her parents and celebrate. I hope we'll enjoy one another and be able to stay clear of interference with our children's wishes.

The wedding … I never did feel quite comfortable with formal things – don't have an awful lot of rules and "oughts" about these things. But, it'll be O K. Those two kids want everyone to have a part in their day; already they've doled out tasks according to everyone's gifts. Have faith, I tell myself. It needs to be their wedding, and we need to help make it the joy they wish.

Visiting them in their home – will I be helpful but not intrusive? My own experience with in-laws was sometimes difficult. It's hard to walk that line.

"I can hardly wait to all go shopping together!" the young bride-to-be was painting future pictures with "moms" and "daughters" planning happy excursions. I guess that's O K.

What are these strange mixtures of feelings racing through my spirit? It's not as if we weren't expecting the announcement. Surely, I should have been prepared to sail right through this. But I'm not. There are tears. They've actually chosen to walk their lives together! They believe in family, in the future, in one another, in the support of those around who love them. It's unbelievable!

There are squeamish insecurities. Will we be able to love them enough to support their marriage? Will we be good in-laws? Will we have the wisdom to speak when we must and be silent when we should? There are soaring dreams. Their future floats around them filled with hope and possibility. What course will they chart? Where will their decisions lead them? Have we done our parent job so they can walk steadily along their way?

There are "next phase" wonderings: Where will we go in our own relationship? What new dreams will we weave? Will the future be kind?

What strange thoughts and feelings cascade around us. All precipitated by one, solemn telephone call. It was like a knock on the door to tomorrow.

Weddings: Where's Love?

WHEN OUR CHILDREN MARRY, we must bless them and send them on their way richer in the hope of future success. Regrettably, this is not what we are encouraged to do. The idea of parents blessing their children never even comes up. Instead, we are told that our energies must be channelled into "doing it just exactly right" and spending lots of money we don't have.

Weddings shouldn't have to bankrupt families. That's what my heart and my life experience tell me.

I've heard horror stories from those who have undergone this passage into their children's family-starting with pain and indebtedness. Price tags of $17,000 to $22,000 seem a high cost for launching these young people into a world beset by unemployment and economic depression.

As I wander through bookstores I see more and more displays of bridal guides spelling out in the most minute detail every proper procedure needed to accomplish the best wedding ever conceived.

My cynical voice whispers, "You don't suppose these guides were financed by interests that benefit directly from their contents?" It seems that a lot of people have their hands out for a piece of the wedding cake!

Movies like "Father of the Bride" expose the heartbreaking and wallet-busting hoops through which a dad must jump to get his beloved daughter married. Although billed as a comedy, it plays far better as a tragedy. The poor guy never had a chance!

Dad cherished her, wanted only the best for her, and, ironically, paid the painful price of never having gotten the chance to bestow his blessing on her union!

Here comes that little voice again: "Don't you know that it's the splash that counts? You've just *got* to have the very best that money can buy. If you really love your children, hang the expense! Or the whole world will know how cheap you are – Humiliation City!"

One of the things I do when I'm not working with families, young people, and staff in our agency is play the organ. Couple after harried couple enter my home weeks ahead of the event to hear and select just the right music for their ceremony. They are almost never happy.

My heart cries out for them. Some have the blessings of family support and assurance; others know that inter-family happiness is only a dim hope for them. Everyone is on someone else's back over ceremonial details, invitations, absent/divorced parent attendance and roles, food selections, flowers, tuxes, honeymoon, reception site, and on and on.

This would all be tolerable if it magically guaranteed marital success. But it doesn't even factor into the equation. Some who eloped after a brief acquaintance did a better job at marriage than those who dated for six years, sustained an engagement for another seven, and spent $40K on a wedding which was indisputably perfect.

Something's missing. Could it be love?

I've witnessed hundreds of weddings over the years and I've always been curious about this: Is it possible to tell before a wedding whether a couple will make it?

I have had some musings on the matter: Does the couple seem to engage in a comfortable give-and-take when they make decisions? Do they enjoy one another? Do they appreciate those who surround them? Are they "giving" folk? Are they strong and unified in their convictions about what values they most want to project throughout the preparations?

Some weddings are gargantuan; others I've seen have involved only 20 people. When the entire bridal party *and* all the guests arrive in two stretch limos, I'm impressed.

Because of its details, each wedding is different, special. It's keyed by the atmosphere the bride and groom most want to communicate. If it's one of joy, celebration and hospitality, I'm convinced the union has a fighting chance at success.

Throwing money around doesn't cut it. Money doesn't bless. It gets spent, and then the bills come, nothing more. It says little about how much the couple is loved or supported in its commitment.

Giving of ourselves to make the day wonderful is what loving is about ... time, talents, advice and counsel, laughter and celebration, surprise, delight, warmth ... and maybe a great loaf of homemade bread.

Mom and four of her friends cooked all the food that fed our 125 guests gathered in the donated church hall. It was the wedding of the decade! It was graceful and loving and generous. But it didn't cost a lot. It blessed everyone instead.

Weddings should be a call to arms – one another's!

Let's try to remember what we're hoping to do through the process. Don't we really want to bless the creation of a new family and all its promise? Don't we want to celebrate the two wonderful adult children who have bravely chosen to say "Yes" to one another?

New In-Law Communications

WHAT'S IT LIKE to be a parent-in-law? I'm wondering because I'm going to be one, so I have lots of question. Maybe my questions are not the right ones, but I'm asking anyway because something in me is wanting to prepare. I hate the thought of tip-toeing through uncharted terrain.

Parenting is a process of letting go, we are told; despite the pain, it seems to be the appropriate principle to invoke as we watch our days play out.

But how and when and to what extent do parents do this letting-go? Once having accomplished it, how do parents cope with the inevitable feelings of mourning?

I used to marvel at why parents cried during their child's wedding. Having lived only through the diamond-giving part, I still wonder about the "sitting in the first pew" part ... and I'll never get to feel Dad's "trip down the aisle with daughter" part.

"I'm not losing a son; I'm gaining a daughter." This sentiment has always seemed a logical, upbeat, constructive adage well-suited to the New England stoic – stiff upper lip and all that.

But, I fear the reality might be more complex. The new couple consists of two people, each of whom comes from a uniquely different family.

Personal and parental expectations, customs, ways of communicating, non-verbal expression, conceptions of how family and child-rearing should be conducted – all of these are different, too. It's the little things around which the new couple's life is built, a new creation within the larger extended family.

I wonder if the balance of "who's gaining which child and how" can be easily tipped in the living out of the "newly vowed" familial complex. For many members the loss is real, the gain purely a numerical one.

Let's just look at the staying-in-touch rules so crucial in maintaining old and in establishing new relationships. She has never established a regular communication with her folks; so, neither she nor they notice much change after the wedding.

But he and his family talk frequently, deeply, with great vigor. Gradually, as the new couple settles into its communications mix, his mom notices that her telephone doesn't ring as much any more. She misses them both terribly, feels she gets cut short when she calls, and begins to feel hurt.

Dad tells Mom that she ought to tell them how she feels. But she's scared that it'll drive the young couple away or make them feel guilty and angry, so she "stuffs" her feelings. Little by little her bricks get laid into a wall, and an obstacle takes shape. Each attempt at communication brings the potential of one more brick.

"The wife is supposed to make all the family contacts," a friend tried to explain. "If the bride doesn't stay in touch with both families, it's probably not going to happen."

"It's been five weeks since I've heard from them," an older mom sighed. Many years had passed since her son's marriage. "I didn't want to be a pest and keep ringing them. So, I stopped; and I got silence in return. I hope they're alright." Worry.

"You never visit us," the young wife lamented, hurt and rejected over her in-laws' regular excuses at her invitations. "If we want to see you we must always travel to your home. Is there something wrong with our hospitality that you don't want to come?"

Whose home hosts the holidays? Both families have large Christmases, so the young couple travels during the entire holiday. Everybody's exhausted, and before long December becomes a family dread.

Negotiate, compromise, cooperate, bend and flex, don't take offense, treat hurts as misunderstandings waiting to be clarified: these efforts make the linking of two families a bit easier. Necessary though these may be, however, these six skills require still another, a keystone, upon which to build: the commitment to communicate. Tough one, that!

If communicating were just a matter of saying words, it wouldn't be so hard to accomplish. But it's a lot more than just words. Anyone who has ever attempted to penetrate another's lifetime of thinking about things in a way different from theirs knows what a monumental task lies at hand.

Beneath the choosing of our words are the feelings, memories, emotional triggers, ancient buttons pushed multiple times, cultural and family attitudes, "right ways of doing things," political and religious tenets, personal styles and tones of voice, non-verbal expressions, moods of the moment, general health and circumstance, economic and employment conditions, time of day, prior happenings of the day, unresolved stress and even weather conditions!

In the midst of these incredible obstacles to clear communications, I wonder how we ever manage to carry on. But we do. And we laugh, struggle, keep trying – because life and family are worth it.

Wedding Pictures

SKY OVERCAST, tropical gusts spiral around old church walls; steeple vaguely outlined in corals and grays and reds. Rehearsal night. Foods spread with color and fragrance and linen cloths and candles.

A blessing time. Gathered together, holding flickering lights, blessing the couple with their love shared. A toast. Joy and nervousness and anticipation.

Family Bible with memories of those who came before. Both sides now, a new family begins. Clothe it well with generations of tradition.

Feasting, laughter, a brand new closeness.

Candlelight glowing the warmth of faces young and not so young, all loving and watching and caring. New friends finding each another, old ones discovering lost connections.

Hand-drawn wedding card from the youngest one ... "Happy Marriage ... I will miss you ... Love, Ben."

Food not eaten bestowed on the hungry at a nearby shelter; brothers spark joy in the packing and delivering. Crews in the tiny kitchen washing, drying; folding warmed chairs and tables; lingering, reluctant to end the magic, gathering candles and ribbons and cloths.

The fresh, new day breaks New England brisk. Feet running about attending to last minute calls and details and touches. Hair curling, makeup, nails, tuxes emerging from black casings, shiny shoes.

Boutonnieres, gardenias, hat pins not working, bending, crooked. Grandma's coming! Her slow walk majestic, solemn, proud.

They're here! Organ swelling: stark, bold music flooding the vaulted nave. Slowly, quietly they come in well-spaced file toward the groom and his men.

A pause. Tall, regal, radiant she comes to a new chord. Father steadies her and reassures. The veil lifted, a kiss.... She moves to her lover's side. May it ever be so.

Vows spoken sure, strong, eyes locked in commitment and love. Rings presented as the gifts tendered. Flowers bestowed on loving parents....

Startling and plaintive, a clear sound cuts the air ... "Flower Song" stuns listeners, breaks tears through dry eyes, speaks love as only a dearly loved brother can. What a gift! Every muscle strains sound through the reluctant horn.

It's too beautiful to contain! Celebrants spill joy in festive exclamation.

Flashes, repositionings, posings, the first toast ... a moment to re-ground with earth once more. Heaven's not a place meant for us ... our souls can't yet contain its glory.

Reception. They're all gathered, waiting, what's next? Chattering, meeting, connecting, introducing, nibbling, sipping, merrymaking.

But the band! It's not here! Guests are, though. What to do? Heart stoppage. Call! Find out! Have they not remembered? Is the car broken and down somewhere on its trek from the City? Quick! Do something! Without music it's gone, over.

The piano sits watching, waiting for someone to light. That's it! Do sit down and play, Mom! The ivories need no urging. Soft, caressing tones mingle with the quiet conversations. It's going to be a party, after all; we'll make it hospitable and warm. Don't worry, please. All will be well.

Laughter. "Where's the brandy glass for tips?"

"No tips today. It's a gift I give."

Plentiful food; heaven sent grace; cordiality.

They're here! Van blew an air hose, but the band's here! Let

the dancing begin, and how! Guitar, drums, keyboard, vocalist –
jazz!

"Dad knew before the rest of us that you two would be standing here! Yours is a great love. It's one I look to imitate." Brother's toast rings clear and sure. He plays for them ... "Someday My
Prince Will Come."

Friends encircle the couple, filling the floor, adding numbers,
growing. How clearly they feel the love in everyone's embrace ...
all dancing together, stretching to gather more and more into the
circle, wordlessly pledging support, confirmation, reception into
the new confraternity of family ... spinning around, laughing at
the unexpected joy.

They're married.

"Let the Lord watch between me and thee when we are separated one from the other."

A Family Tragedy

SOMEWHERE in a large New England city hospital a young mother awaits the birth of her first child. Her labor is about to begin, and she is frightened at the prospect.

All is in readiness. The young woman who is her coach stands by ready for the onset. Those who know of her and her peculiar circumstances also stand ready to receive word of the birth.

This birth is different from most. She conceived this child at the mercy of a man she knew for just three hours. On the way home from their chance meeting he forced himself on her, leaving her shaken and pleading. It soon became clear she was pregnant.

In her mid-twenties, she is already launched in her career. She holds a college diploma, with distinction. Her position with a reputable company is secure. But she has lived in hell the past nine months, guarding her secret and telling only a few trusted friends.

What to do? Her initial confusion at the news of her pregnancy threw her into a whirlwind of choices, none of which would leave her or her baby free from pain.

Whether or not to abort the baby compelled her to face making her first choice. Investigating thoroughly, both with those who know her soul and with those whose medical expertise she values, she chose to say "No."

Without even considering the adoption choice, she readied herself to fill the role of single mom. She knew the path as well as she was able without actually having lived it.

Yes, she could earn good money to support her tiny family; but she would need to make major parental compromises to sustain her breadwinner status. What if she were asked to travel? The long hours she already knew were required of her position would keep her from raising the child and witnessing his milestones. The more she thought the deeper her discouragement became.

When the time came to tell her son about his father, what could she tell him? That he'd raped her? That his father violated his mother and so brought about his existence? It would be a lonely, heavy burden ... a burden for life with traps yet uncharted.

Adoption. What about that? Surely there were warm and loving couples ready for the commitment of a long sought-after child to raise and nurture.

That's what she'd do! She'd give this precious child a full and rich life with an already-formed family.

She searched and asked around and sought professional recommendations and found an adoption agency. As her time drew near, she chose the couple who would get the news of her impending delivery. No, she couldn't bear to meet them face-on-face, but they sounded wonderful on paper.

Her mourning deepened. As she composed the letter which would be delivered to the child at the appropriate age, she wept. She wept, too, as she cross-stitched the beautiful sampler going with the letter to the baby's new home. It got so she wept almost constantly.

And the baby grew under her disciplined self-care. Those around her saw how she spoke to the baby, rubbing her belly and soothing the little one as it tumbled within her. She stopped drinking coffee; not a drop of alcohol crossed her young lips; she took her vitamins, kept her diet lean and maintained a vigorous regimen of exercise.

She waits now for the newborn squeal, knowing it'll all be over soon. Labor has begun.

But she tightly holds a doubt in the secret places of her heart. Her rigidly constructed logic compels her to sustain the decision she has made over the past few months. She can't disappoint that couple now waiting, too, but in the privacy of their home – waiting for news of their new child's birth.

She awaits release now. There's no happy anticipation in that hospital room. Joy has not been a guest in her home for nine months. Her hopes and dreams, her emptiness, her sorrow have all become one with her spirit.

Parents, family, friends, those who love her, mourn deeply the tragedy of her rape and what it has brought in its wake. Life as it had been will never come again, for any of them. The baby hasn't shown his tiny face yet. She hasn't seen him or held him or given him to the adoption worker for the next step. Final papers have not yet been signed. All these pieces lie ahead.

Tragedies such as this one can visit any family. When they do, we are asked to stand by and hug and cry together and listen hard to the loved one who most needs us now.

This young mother's final decision will soon be made, and she'll begin her long years of recovery. Her loved ones will try to heal each other's wounds as best they can. And they'll wonder at the meaning of it all.

Daring to Dream

D REAMS GIVE new life to the discouraged," explained the director of an innovative participatory theater troupe. He and his thespians have for many years served only those who were incarcerated at local prisons. During his public radio interview he reported how the theatrical presentations had affected inmates. Convicts had changed the directions of their past lives into new, creative and productive ones.

"To be human means to dream," he went on. "Dreams set directions, raise hopes and release the energy needed to do the work which must follow."

It's not just the profoundly discouraged who need to dream. It's all of us.

Some who read this book are acquainted with the Upper Room's TIPS (Teen Information for Parenting Success) Project. Its purpose is to provide peer group support, community connections and multi-faceted instruction to young families struggling with establishing themselves in the world.

When individuals inquire about this project, they frequently ask its goals. Of the three that steer TIPS, one in particular evokes a startled response: "To reconnect the teens with their dreams." Upon hearing it, questioners often sigh, smile and ponder.

It's a goal which is "unexpected" by most standards; but, it's critical to the program's widespread success.

Every two months or so, I sit with these young parents and ask, "What's your dream?" Everyone is given time to answer; we encourage one another to speak out our dream, but it's a hard thing to do. Saying it aloud gives it a reality. That might mean we might have to do something about it, and maybe it won't come together, and then we'll be hurt, and we know all about being hurt.

Everyone has to participate, though, even first-time visitors, friends, staff, moms and dads, even me.

The dreams seem to explode from the speakers' mouths.

One young woman told us she'd finally found her birth father last week. Now she's dreaming about getting her driver's license. As she spoke, a driving instructor entered the room and offered to teach her. Already she's had one lesson and plans to drive on her own before the end of the summer.

Right in the middle of a guest speaker's presentation, another young mom whispered to me that she was going to get her GED.

"Of course you are!" I hushed, trying to get her attention back to the gentleman busy making a critical point at the blackboard.

"No, you don't understand," she was getting frustrated with my put-off. "I really *am* going to get it!" I nodded, looking incredulously at her earnest face.

Today she holds her certificate. Completed. In September she'll be starting college. Everything's all set; she's received her acceptance letter, the money she needs, her childcare allowance.

One day a TIPS mom already in college came to a teen parent meeting with her own startling discovery: "I think I know why we're all having difficulty in our relationships with our men. We've dreamed our dreams and are doing them, but they're not. They watch, hold down two or three jobs to support our families, and wonder when their turn will come. They know there's no extra money for classes and books and GED test fees. There's barely enough for food."

"So, what should we do?" I wanted to hear her idea.

"Can't we put together some GED tutorials for them during our Wednesday night meetings?" she looked hopeful.

"Of course we can!" I sounded more confident than I felt. I should have known from long experience that where there's a will there's a way.

And so it has come to pass. Through the dedicated efforts of several area educators the sessions have begun and will continue through the summer. Every volunteer who's taught one of these has returned home after an evening with the young men glowing, exhilarated, unable to stop chattering about the eagerness with which the young fathers have undertaken their task.

I've had dreams, too. Ever since college I've wanted to do two things before I die: visit the Louvre Museum in Paris and fly in an untethered hot air balloon. Five years ago my son Chris and I met at DeGaulle Airport before his return home from a semester abroad, and we "did" that magnificent museum. When I saw "Venus de Milo" I unabashedly wept my tears of joy and gratitude.

Not long after, I accomplished my second dream. As five balloon passengers we rose gently off the ground in our snug basket. We viewed the shrinking figures of our loved ones waving their "Bon Voyages" down below. None of us could speak. Each of us had dreamed this dream, and someone who loved us made it come true. How can words be spoken at a time like that?

Everyone needs to dream, regardless of age. We must dare. And we must ask one another to speak those dreams. It's important to give dreams birth, reality. This done, we must fan one another's dreams into flame. That's what loved ones are for, to help life get lived through dreams getting dreamed and hopes coming true.

Dare to Feel

HUGH DOWNS, in a televised interview with Marian Christy, spoke eloquently about his dedication to the numerous environmental and humanitarian causes he has espoused over the years:

"My commitment is whole-hearted and total; it's not just an intellectual one. The mind is only one of the tools which serves the heart. Feelings, spirituality, ethical values, the physical realm … these, too, play their significant roles."

His posture was soft, reflective, gentle. The whole, entire man spoke through his visual self; he communicated his powerful completeness and integration. He seemed to know who he was, and he rested peacefully with it; yet, he struggled deep within, to answer the questions, probing and personal. The work was hard.

As I watched, I felt magnetically drawn to him. Somehow I sensed that, in the midst of the public career into which he had been thrown, he had managed to retain a large measure of his humanity and serenity. The highly competitive and often cut-throat broadcasting field he'd chosen had frequently left him on the outside looking in; but, he continued getting work because key program professionals knew who he was and that they wanted him.

Was he threatened by Barbara Walters' formidable screen presence on their popular show? Hardly. It was an ability to complement each other that had given their partnership such value to the program, he asserted.

He'd done his work well. He seemed to be in touch with who he was. This enabled him to let others be themselves, as well. It was his "work of the heart" that bestowed the success. And it gave him peace, at least some of the time.

I began thinking about the people all around, those whom I love, struggling to accomplish the same sensitivity and wholeness in their lives. I wondered if their vulnerability was getting them anywhere and if it was worth their pain.

"Can you believe that I didn't even have a vocabulary for my feelings until just a few years ago?" It was a gentleman in his late 30s who spoke. "Imagine my confusion when emotions erupted within me, and I didn't know what was happening and felt I would soon explode."

But he kept them inside, terrified to act on them, afraid to go to the edge and lose control. His internal pressure built, and his spirit floated in and out of madness. He reached out for help and ultimately began to sort through the maze of undefined emotions that colored his life.

As I heard his story I wept inside at humankind's inability to give those we love either the vocabulary or the permission to feel. Those who eventually discover its fascinating dimensions are inevitably transformed by them. And they pass it on.

They find that reality becomes fuller, more dynamic, fraught with complexities never before understood; they are less able to tolerate black-white thinking and are more prone to listen and bend with the insights of others.

But learning how to feel is scary. And it's hard work. And it makes life more difficult. And it usually means that more energy must be spent communicating effectively and deeply with others. It lends new meaning to relationships and rejoices in seemingly inconsequential nuances of speech and gesture.

"I can't be bothered with this feeling stuff," she spoke impatiently, "I've got a lot to do, and I need to focus. Getting in touch with how I feel and sharing that with others important to me just gets me off the track."

Quite the contrary. Clarifying our feelings gets us to the very core of meaning. It takes the confused reality out of the inside of our heads and presents it for examination to someone else who cares deeply about and understands us. This process enables our experience to be viewed from a variety of perspectives, frequently reducing it to its proper size and shape.

We need to encourage one another to dare to feel. First, we must give them permission; then, we must give them the words that fit their emotions; and, most critically, we must commit to struggle with them as they attempt to clarify and share them.

If our loved ones short-cut their problems to flee from doing their emotional work, we must urge them back to the task. Life cannot be lived on a single cylinder; every piece of the human person – mind, spirit, body, emotions – must be mobilized to the effort.

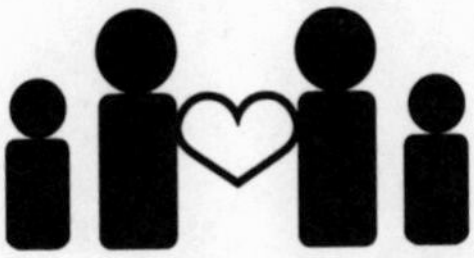

Ten Commandments of Parenting

WHEN THE LIFE of the parent-child relationship needs revitalizing, it's helpful to have a set of reminders and "encouragers" at hand.

With some humility, I present the following for your consideration. The "legalese" happened before I could help myself. It seemed to lend a somewhat more proper tone to this list. I hope this effort will help in the rather overwhelming job of parenting that we are all working so hard to accomplish.

1. Thou shalt watch, wonder at, listen to and seek in every way to know and accept this child who brings visions from another world that are the voices of a new generation.
2. Thou shalt with every effort fill the child's basic needs for love and nurturing: food, clothing and shelter; safety; education; recreation; security; predictability; and spiritual well being.
3. Thou shalt not allow a child to hurt self, others, or property without directly intervening, instructing in the proper care of these, re-directing into appropriate and constructive behaviors and encouraging the repair of any damage.
4. Thou shalt seek in every way possible and with untiring energy to communicate with the child, regardless of the difficulty, while preserving the utmost dignity and respect due a social equal.
5. Thou shalt expect the best and highest of each child as is appropriate to the child's age, experience and circumstance; further, provide encouragement at every child effort, with appreciation and joy.
6. Thou shalt teach with truth, understanding, gentleness, patience and good example the very best and most beautiful mysteries you contain.

7. Thou shalt give real and appropriate choices at every opportunity with the responsibilities attendant to them, understanding that autonomy is central to carrying out these choices, and appreciating that mistakes lie at the core of true learning and discovery.

8. Thou shalt never strike or humiliate or dismiss or violate or exploit or judge the child, but rather consider and honor and treat with precious regard.

9. Thou shalt seek in every way to encourage cooperation within the social unit, nurturing the child's gifts as real and important contributions to the good of that community, and trusting that such a group may provide the support required for the child's growth into adulthood.

10. Thou shalt, regardless of circumstance, "be there" for the child, not to "bail out" but to "stand with," supporting and encouraging and helping the child to face whatever eventuality presents itself.

WHAT LIES BENEATH this rather formidable listing is the understanding that, when we act with respect, good example, dedication to reality, openness, self-control, and attention to good balance, we show how deeply we love the young people we've been privileged to mentor.

Mom's Proverb Is Ever New

B E CAREFUL how you think. Your life is shaped by your thoughts." It's a chorus she sings. Those who know her hear it often. Above her telephone it hangs rendered in carefully wrought needlework. She refers to it repeatedly as she talks with friends, reminding herself and them of the truth she recites.

They listen. Some dismiss this, her own personal proverb, as something they hear often; some strain to understand how it applies to their problems. Some scratch their heads and just don't get it.

It's her hallmark, and they know that. They love her, wonder at her resilience in facing her own life, and suspect she follows her own advice. After all, she's lived out her 86 years without consuming shelves full of medications designed to regulate every bodily function.

How does she twist her thinking around in such ways that she maintains her sparkling smile and quick steps? Life has dealt her countless spirit-shaking blows, but she's kept her balance.

Versatile, nimble, active in community affairs, she's a wonder to those who behold.

Magically, her driveway is the first to get shoveled after snowstorms; her lawn mysteriously gets mowed before she touches the old machine tucked away in her garage. Her neighbors honor her. She can often be seen bringing plates full of fudge or cookies to them; or, perhaps, coloring books with crayons for their children.

She never fails to express surprise at the generosity of others, appreciating their thinking of her, wondering why they seem so eager to help.

"Be careful how you think. Your life is shaped by your thoughts."

Some have capitalized on her particular kind of thinking by writing best-selling books and following up with lengthy, expensive workshops. They know the power of her proverb. They also know how effectively we sabotage our own lives with patterns of thought that defeat success.

Parents under stress destroy both themselves *and* their children by not watching how they think.

"These kids are such brats in the morning! I scream at them from the minute they get up. They move like molasses. You'd think they were trying to make me late for work!" The distraught mom wrung her hands in exasperation.

I think she wanted to just let her feelings out. But I also think she wished she could do her morning routine better. Should I try the proverb on her? It sounded so trite and dumb. After all, her problem was real, and she was stuck in a hole. Her hole looked just like the one in which countless others who work and have young children find themselves.

"Try thinking a whole new way about the dilemma," I said. "Let's see, rather than dreading the coming of morning, why not look forward to it?"

"But that's defying the reality of life as we've lived it so far!" she objects.

"Well, can we for absurdity's sake play out another scenario? The night before, make sure the kids know the next morning's routine, lay out their clothes, and ask what they'd like for breakfast." I knew it had worked for me during a horrendous time in my own life.

"With the coming of day, see if you can get up a bit earlier, shower, and have cup NO. 1 of coffee right away. Put on some lively music, turn on atmospheric lighting, give extra time to finish regular washing up and dressing; when all is humming along nicely, say to yourself, we're actually going to make it this morning! I'm not even going to rush! I'm going to keep my voice soft. The young ones shouldn't have to hear shouting so early." I was still offering suggestions.

"Be real!" she said. Wait! She was laughing. That was a good sign. She'd heard.

Maybe my picture was too far removed from hers. But I was sure she could craft her own picture, one that would work for her as surely as mine had worked for me many years ago.

"Be careful how you think. Your life is shaped by your thoughts."

We can actively choose instead of just acquiescing.

We can decide to have a productive day or wallow in laziness and boredom.

We can plan to take an exploring walk for an hour with our children, or we can completely lose our sanity by loudly insisting they play more quietly.

We can turn a rude gesture from a passing motorist into an enthusiastic wave and smile.

We can look inside ourselves and see worthiness and dignity, or we can see uselessness and failure.

We can abandon our depressing thoughts for an hour to take a mental vacation, or we can cave into their draining influence and let them run our lives.

We can decide to change one attitude that gets in the way of our relationships, or we can imprison ourselves by thinking that who we are is all we can ever be.

About the Author

ANNA WILLIS is a mother of four, musician, educator and program director at The Upper Room, Education for Parenting, Inc. Educated in the sciences and in early childhood education, she has come to be viewed as a "friend of the family" by human service professionals and those she serves.

Anna Willis has been a regular family-issues columnist for the Derry News since 1988.

In 1991, she received the "Woman of the Year" award from the Business Professional Women of New Hampshire.

About the Upper Room

The Upper Room, Education for Parenting, Inc. is a not-for-profit corporation which develops and implements educational programs and services specifically designed to strengthen families.

Founded in 1986 by Claire Hamilton and Anna Willis, the Upper Room has focused much of its work on serving the special needs of adolescents.

Based in Derry, NH, the Upper Room has supported more than 4,000 family members and has received eight national, state and community awards.

· · ·

PROCEEDS FROM THE SALE OF THIS BOOK SUPPORT
UPPER ROOM'S YOUTH AND FAMILY PROGRAMS.

· · ·

Contacting The Upper Room

For information regarding the Upper Room's programs and services or for ordering additional copies of this book, please write or call:

The Upper Room
Education for Parenting, Inc.
Post Office Box 1017
Derry, NH 03038

(603) 437-8477